Irish American
Material Culture

Irish American Material Culture

A DIRECTORY OF COLLECTIONS, SITES, AND FESTIVALS IN THE UNITED STATES AND CANADA

Compiled by
Susan K. Eleuterio-Comer

Material Culture Directories, Number 1

G P

Greenwood Press
New York • Westport, Connecticut • London

Library of Congress Cataloging-in-Publication Data

Eleuterio-Comer, Susan K.
    Irish American material culture : a directory of collections,
sites, and festivals in the United States and Canada / compiled by
Susan K. Eleuterio-Comer.
        p.   cm.—(Material culture directories, ISSN 0743-7528 ; no.
1)
    Bibliography: p.
    Includes index.
    ISBN 0-313-24731-5 (lib. bdg. : alk. paper)
    1. Irish Americans—Material culture—Directories. 2. Irish—
Canada—Material culture—Directories. I. Title. II. Series.
E184.I6E43   1988
305.8′9162′071—dc19   88-11038

British Library Cataloguing in Publication Data is available.

Library of Congress Catalog Card Number: 88-11038
ISBN: 0-313-24731-5
ISSN: 0743-7528

First published in 1988

Greenwood Press, Inc.
88 Post Road West, Westport, Connecticut 06881

Printed in the United States of America

∞

The paper used in this book complies with the
Permanent Paper Standard issued by the National
Information Standards Organization (Z39.48-1984).

10 9 8 7 6 5 4 3 2 1

Contents

Series Foreword   vii

Preface   ix

Acknowledgments   xiii

Introduction: Irish-American History from 1600   xv

Chapter I: Collections   3

Chapter II: National Register Sites   51

Chapter III: Festivals   69

Appendix: Selected List of Irish Sources   85

Bibliography   89

Name Index   93

General Index   99

Series Foreword

In the past twenty-five years, the United States and Canada
have seen a great upsurge of interest in ethnicity. This
interest was first fueled by the civil rights movement in
the United States and the move toward multi-culturalism in
Canada. It has been rekindled by the United States
Bicentennial, the publication and broadcast of Roots,
and the centennial of the Statue of Liberty. It has spawned
journals and newsletters, national organizations, special
libraries, and festivals. It has been equally popular with
academics and the general public.
        Interest in the study of material culture, as a means
of explicating traditional and popular culture, has also
grown steadily in recent years. Since 1980, journals and
newsletters have been founded to disseminate ideas about
material culture studies, monographs and anthologies of
major articles have been published, and museums large and
small are taking a more careful, culturally based approach
to the interpretation of their collections.
        The Greenwood Press series of Material Culture
Directories brings together the study of ethnicicty and
material culture. Modeled on Greenwood's Museums, Sites,
and Collections of Germanic Culture in North America
(compiled by Margaret Hobbie, 1980), the series is the first
concerted effort to locate and describe ethnic material
culture and photographic collections in the United States
and Canada. Many directories in the series will go beyond
the German volume by including chapters on festivals, which
in some communities afford outsiders the best--often the
sole--access to a group's material culture.
        Each volume in itself raises fundamental questions
about the role of material culture in ethnic identity--what
has been preserved, by whom, where, and why? But the series
is not meant to stand alone. It is, rather, an attempt to
facilitate further studies on the role of material culture
in the lives of North American ethnic communities--studies
of the signs and symbols that help establish ethnic
identity, or studies of "everyday" material culture and the
extent to which it reflects traditional or mainstream
values.
        The compilers hope, as well, that the series will

encourage ethnic communities to begin to look at their past
in terms of their material culture. They hope that history
museums and other potential repositories will collaborate
with local ethnic communities in initiating or increasing
efforts to collect objects and photographs that reflect the
ethnic experience.

     This directory on Irish collections by Susan
Eleuterio-Comer is the first volume in the series to appear.
These entries were particularly difficult to assemble
because of the widespread opinion among the non-Irish (and
some Irish) that Irish-Americans and Irish-Canadians have
been totally assimilated into their mainstream cultures; the
slowness by most Irish communities in establishing
historical societies and museums; and the failure of
collections that do hold Irish materials to identify them as
such. Nonetheless, Eleuterio-Comer has compiled a long list
of Irish-American and Irish-Canadian repositories and
festivals, creating an important new tool for research on
Irish immigration. We hope that this volume will help that
list to grow.

                                        Margaret Hobbie
                                        Series Editor

Preface

Studies of Irish immigrants to North America and their
descendants have until recently used conventional methods of
historical research and focused on conventional subjects.
They have relied for the most part on written sources. Their
subject matter has concentrated on politics and religion and
the famous men associated with these subjects.

More recent studies, cited in the bibiliography, have
focused on the role of Irish immigrant women, particularly
after the Great Famine immigration (Hasia Diner); the
interaction of the Irish with regional cultures (Dennis
Clark); and sociological and psychological perceptions of
the immigrants (Kerby Miller). These new studies have drawn
on more varied source material such as letters, diaries and
oral interviews.

Historians, folklorists, cultural geographers and
others are now seeking to use physical objects as sources of
immigrant history as well. These include buildings,
photographs, household objects, tools, musical instruments,
and clothing; created, brought, or transformed by members of
particular ethnic groups. This study seeks to make some of
these objects, the material culture of the Irish, more
accessible to researchers of Irish-American and
Irish-Canadian history and culture through a descriptive
listing of locations where such materials can be found.
Festivals have been included because they are frequently the
most comprehensive sites of both historical and contemporary
Irish-American culture.

The emphasis of this directory is on non-bibliographic
materials, although outstanding book or other written
material collections are noted where relevant.
Irish-Americans are considered here as groups rather than as
individuals so that collections which relate only to one
specific person, such as President John F. Kennedy, are not
included.

The collections, sites, and festivals described are
divided into three groups. Chapter I describes the
Irish-American holdings of ninety museums, libraries,
historical societies, archives, and centers in the United
States and Canada. These descriptions note objects,

historical photographs, ephemera, buildings, and oral
history. Chapter II abstracts forty-four relevant sites
from the 1976 edition of The National Register of Historic
Places (with some later additions to the register). Many
of the listed sites are historic churches and houses, but
schools, neighborhoods, and monuments are included as well.
Also listed are monuments in Canada. Chapter III lists
twenty-seven festivals in the United States and Canada with
a brief history of each festival and a description of its
events, including documentation available to researchers.
An appendix lists collections in Ireland.

Margaret Hobbie in her preface to Museums, Sites, and
Collections of Germanic Culture in North America (1980)
describes the limitations of the study of material culture
in terms of criticality. She defines the criticality of an
object as the "extent to which it expresses its historical
and cultural context." One factor which has limited the
collection of Irish-American objects is the fact that most
Irish immigrants either arrived as English speakers or had
become English-speaking by the time they could afford to
leave objects for posterity. Many curators have noted in
their responses to the survey for this directory that they
were sure there must be objects in their collection with an
Irish-American connection, but the connection had not been
established. Irish-American objects are difficult to
identify in part because of the lack of a "foreign language"
to signify their ethnicity. Collections have been included
in this directory even though their connection to
Irish-American culture remains to be established. A note
warning that prior research is necessary is included with
these listings.

Criticality is limited by such factors as aesthetic
value, physical strength of any particular object, attitudes
of curators towards Irish-American materials, and
traditional attitudes towards objects in the larger
Irish-American community. While the Irish have long been
recognized for their oral tradition and later their interest
and ability in literature, their tradition has not
emphasized collection of material objects. This has been
due to a combination of economic factors, a political
history of repression, and perhaps to the prejudice faced by
the Irish both in their own country under the English and in
the United States. At the same time however, studies done
in this century have documented the unique nature of Irish
culture, including buildings, land use, and objects, (Estyn
Evans, Kevin O'Sullivan, Henry Glassie). Such studies
remain to be done on the material culture of the Irish in
North America except for the fine work of John Mannion in
Eastern Canada. There have been a number of exhibits on
local Irish-American history and these are noted with the
collections.

The collections of Irish-American organizations, such
as the United Irish Cultural Center in San Francisco and the
American Irish Historical Society in New York, provide many
Irish-American materials. As in most historical studies of
the Irish however, these collections tend to emphasize the
achievements of outstanding individuals and wealthier
members of the community. Collections in general historical
agencies actually seem to include a broader range of

historical periods and levels of culture, for example,
materials at the Balch Institute in Philadelphia and at the
Chicago Historical Society, which include everyday objects
such as quilts, toys, clothing, and school desks. Even
here, however, there is an emphasis on certain periods of
Irish-American history--represented through numerous
broadsides depicting eighteenth and nineteenth century
stereotyped views of the Irish immigrants. A few collections
of individuals willing to be contacted by researchers have
been included because so many materials remain in private
possession. Most Irish fraternal and social organizations
have not yet seen the need to place objects documenting
their history and traditions into public collections.
Several curators indicate an interest in collecting more
Irish material, and it is to be hoped that this volume will
encourage donations to museums and historical societies.

The collections included in this directory were chosen
through a variety of methods. About two hundred
questionnaires were sent to potential repositories during
1984-1987. The names of these institutions were selected
from other directories, such as the Official Museum
Directory and the Directory of Historical Agencies in
the United States and Canada , or suggested by manuscript
sources of Irish-American works and Irish-American
researchers whose advice was solicited. Festivals were
selected from Irish-American newspapers and guides to
Irish-American culture (see Bibliography). Some
collections and festivals may have been missed due to the
difficulty of locating Irish-American collections and the
somewhat ephemeral nature of contacts for festivals. In
addition, some potentially relevant collections and
festivals did not respond to the questionnaire or to
follow-up queries.

Acknowledgments

A discussion about the existence of Irish-American culture
with Margaret Hobbie led to this volume. It is directly
based on her work Museums, Sites, and Collections of
Germanic Culture in North America. The groundwork laid by
that volume in its use of questionnaires and method of
creating categories for ethnic material culture is
invaluable. I am very grateful to Margaret and to Cynthia
Harris and Lynn Flint at Greenwood Press for their
assistance during the time it has taken to compile this
material.

Many individuals helped with this work and in
particular I want to thank Bob Burns, Angela Carter, Dennis
Clark, John Concannon, John Corrigan, Michael Funchion,
Peter Kenny, Mary O'Reilly, Dennis Ryan, Father Michael
Quinlan, Ellen Skerrett, and John Traynor for their
suggestions for resources and categories. Thanks also go to
the many curators, librarians, and other staff who promptly
and carefully answered the questionnaire and my phone
inquiries. Donna Christiansen, John Dowd, Roger Haydon, and
Margaret Hobbie helped produce the manuscript in several
ways and I appreciate their help as well.

Most of all, I thank my husband, Christopher Comer, not
only for his constant support and encouragement, but also
for rolling up his sleeves and designing ways to elicit
information from his fellow Irishmen and women. Credit for
completion of this work goes to him with much gratitude and
love.

Finally, I must thank Thomas and Mary Comer and Herb
and Marianne Eleuterio for their gracious support and
encouragement throughout the creation of this book. It is
dedicated to them and to Colin, Sarah, Joseph and Patrick
with hopes that it will add to their Irish heritage.

INTRODUCTION

Irish-American History from 1600

BACKGROUND

In this work, the term "Irish-American" includes immigrants and their descendants from the present-day Republic of Ireland and Northern Ireland who have settled in North America during the past four centuries. It draws in Irish-Americans of all religious denominations from Roman Catholics to Irish Presbyterians, Episcopalians, Methodists, Quakers, Baptists, and Jews. It also encompasses those people whose ancestors were known as "Scotch-Irish" (or Ulster Scots) and who emigrated to the United States and Canada from northern Ireland during the seventeenth century and later for economic and religious reasons.

These immigrants, unlike many other ethnic groups in North America, were linked not by a "foreign" language but by their culture of origin and by a history which consistently included religious repression and economic discrimination. While there have been many periods of factionalism among Irish immigrants and their descendants, there has also been a long history of joint participation by Protestants and Catholics in particularly "Irish" groups and causes. These date from such benevolent societies as the Charitable Irish Society of Boston (established in 1737) and the Hibernian Society of Charleston, South Carolina (established in 1799), and have continued up to today with political and social groups related to the "troubles" in Northern Ireland, such as the Ulster Project (begun in 1975) which brings Catholic and Protestant teenagers from Northern Ireland to the United States for recreation and education during the summer.

Ireland's history has been one of continual invasion followed by absorption of the invaders. The present day Irish are descendants of Celts, Vikings, Normans, English, and Scots. In 1166, "the king of Leinster (the easternmost of the original four provinces of Ireland) invited Norman Lords from Wales to assist him against his rival Ruaidri O Conehubhair, the high King of Ireland (1)." This was the beginning of a long and bitter relationship between the English and the Irish which has not ended to this day. From this time until 1600, the Irish, particularly those outside the area around Dublin called the Pale, continued to

maintain their traditional way of life which included a
system of rules and customs called the Brehon Laws, a strong
and unique form of Christianity, and a political system of a
number of fiefdoms ruled by clan leaders who often fought
with one another. After a succession of attacks on these
leaders by the English during the 1500s, Ireland came under
complete English control after the battle of Kinsale in
1601. With this control came the prohibition of the Brehon
Laws; the establishment of "plantations" of Protestants
(mostly Scotch Presbyterians) in Ulster, the northern
province of Ireland; and the attempt by the English to
transform what had been a "pastoral, and
subsistence-oriented Irish rural" Catholic society to a
commercially based, Anglican, English colony (2). Under
Cromwell in the 1640s, Catholics were murdered in some cases
and forced into indenture as servants in many others. A
series of restrictive penal laws were enacted during the
late 1600s and early 1700s which stripped Catholics of
virtually all rights, including land ownership, and which
increased rents and led to the persecution of all dissenters
from the Anglican Church. These laws created a class of
"emigrants and exiles" who fled the country in steadily
increasing numbers. One scholar has noted that "between
1600 and 1800, almost everyone in Ireland had reason to look
beyond the island for a more favorable habitat (3)."

EMIGRATION TO THE NEW WORLD

Large scale Irish emigration to North America dates from
soon after the establishment of a Scottish "plantation" in
Ulster in 1607. From this time until the end of the
century, Irish emigration was primarily Catholic. Beginning
with settlers who arrived in Virginia in the 1620s, Irish
immigrants seeking relief from the economic and religious
restrictions of British rule came to the West Indies and the
American Colonies. Most were drawn to the religiously
tolerant colonies of Virginia and Maryland during the first
part of the century. Thousands more were shipped to the
islands and the colonies as indentured servants. During the
1650s, Irish fishermen began seasonal migrations to the
banks of Newfoundland (Pre-Federation Canada), laying the
groundwork for eventual migration of Irish immigrants to
this area as well. Pennsylvania gradually replaced Virginia
and Maryland as the American colony of choice during the
later part of the century due to restrictions against
Catholics passed during the 1690s.
      Little is known about the social history of these early
Irish immigrants. Dennis Clark points out that "the Irish
who came to the earliest white man's America were the
poorest of the colonial immigrants (4)." While there were a
few early schemes to establish settlements of Irish in
Virginia, New England, and Maryland, none of these
succeeded. The majority of immigrants seem to have been
indentured servants who were often despised for their
nationality and religion. While a few individuals became
wealthy landowners, many more remained poor and in servitude
or ran away to become frontier dwellers along the
Appalachians from Pennsylvania south to the Carolinas (5).

Because of growing resistance in the American Colonies towards Catholics, and the restrictions of the Penal Laws in Ireland, Irish immigration during the 1700s was dominated by Protestants. While many of these were Ulster Scots, there were also a number of Quakers and Episcopalians. These immigrants settled mostly from Pennsylvania south through Maryland, Virginia, the Carolinas and Georgia. They primarily seem to have become farmers and were considered to be quite independent and "impatient with authority (6)." During the latter part of the century Irish craftsmen such as furniture makers and silversmiths came to urban areas like Philadelphia. Recent studies have begun to examine the influence of these craftsmen on early American design (7).

By the American Revolution, "most Irish Presbyterian emigrants and their descendants were still 'Ulster-Americans' whose customs and attitudes reflected a practical synthesis of cultural retentions, borrowings and adaptions (8)." Kerby Miller in his work on Irish emigrants notes that the Ulster Scots material culture in the 1700's was a mix of traditional practices such as growing flax and weaving linen, and innovations such as the log cabin of the Germans and Swedes in which they "reshaped the floor plan to that of a traditional Ulster farmhouse." He goes on to note, "even their music was a blend of Ulster Scottish, Native Irish, and Anglo-American forms (9)." Recent controversial scholarship by Gardy McWhiney and Forrest McDonald (called the Celtic Thesis) postulates that these immigrants along with other Protestants from Ireland and their descendants had a tremendous cultural effect on the South quite different from the portrait painted by most historians of the Scotch-Irish (10). This portrait emphasized the conservative, entreprenurial, and highly religious nature of this group and concentrated on those individuals who played an important role in the American Revolution and the early American government. Leroy V. Eid has detailed the contrast between this traditional description and the "wild" independent and unruly Irish described by the Celtic Thesis (11). The Irish influence on the South during the eighteenth century is likely to be studied and argued about for some time. What cannot be denied is that many immigrants from Ireland were actively involved in the American revolution and in shaping both the urban and rural communities which grew out of the colonies.

Between 1820-1845 over one million Irish came to North America. It is difficult to estimate exactly how many of those came to Canada, but most historians agree that the majority who landed in Canada continued to the United States for their permanent residence. The Irish-Canadians tended to become farmers and most of them were Protestant, although there were significant numbers of Irish Catholics. The major areas of settlement in Canada were the Maritime Provinces-Newfoundland, New Brunswick, and Prince Edward Island-, Quebec, and Ontario. Although there were tensions in Canada between Catholics and Protestants, the fact that the Irish immigrants were British subjects like the Pre-Federation Canadians meant that a "nativist" anti-Catholic movement never developed there as it did for a time in the United States.

Irish immigration gradually became more heavily Catholic and more directed towards urban areas. By 1800, "Philadelphia was the most heavily Irish city in America, a mix of Quakers, Presbyterians, Episcopalians, and Catholics (12)." Tensions between Protestants and Catholics increased during the first half of the century and Philadelphia was torn by violent riots during 1844. These "intra-Irish" riots were preceded and followed by anti-Catholic riots in other parts of the country, led by mobs of nativist Americans called "Know Nothings (13)." Especially after the 1840's, the Irish in the United States tended to stay in the urban centers of the East Coast-Philadelphia, Boston, New York, and Newark- or to migrate to other cities, especially Chicago, St. Louis, St. Paul, New Orleans, and San Francisco. However, recent scholars of Irish-American history have stressed the dispersal of the Irish in fairly large numbers throughout the United States because of their work on railroads and canals, in mines, and in the army. One scholar has gone so far as to estimate that as many as 40 percent of the Irish immigrants actually became rural dwellers, and another, John Ridge, has traced the history of Ancient Order of Hibernian lodges throughout the States, including Alaska, Hawaii, and also in Mexico. Most scholars agree, however, that the majority of the Irish were urban dwellers and the influence of Irish-American history and culture has been most evident in the cities of the East and Midwest and in San Francisco (14).

Two aspects of life in Ireland which must be noted for their influence on the immigrants and their descendants are the Great Famine of 1845-1851 and Ireland's drive for independence from Britain. During the first part of the nineteenth century, Irish peasants were subjected to a series of economic and political situations which brought them great distress. The failure of the entire potato crop in 1845 and for several years after was devastating to Ireland's population and had a tremendous effect on the economic and social structure as well. The Irish population dropped by two million during the years 1845-1851 with estimates of one million lost to disease and starvation and another million to emigration, primarily to the United States and Canada. (The only monuments to Irish immigration in this volume are those in Canada which record the deaths of cholera infested famine immigrants who died in Canada before they could turn south to the United States.) These "famine Irish" immigrants had a great impact not only numerically but on Irish-American society as well. Many earlier Protestant Irish immigrants who had been content to be known as Irish now took on the name "Scotch-Irish" in order to distinguish themselves from the wretchedly poor, primarily Catholic, starving Irish who now flooded into North America. During the 1840-1860s, a number of Loyal Orange Institution lodges were founded especially in Pittsburgh, Philadelphia, and New York. These lodges were based on Protestant fraternal societies in Ireland that frequently included violent acts against Catholics in their activities (15). The new immigrants who survived, packed into ghettos on the East Coast, produced a wave of anti-Irish and anti-Catholic hatred in the United States which affected the Irish well into the twentieth century.

     In spite of their poverty, most of the famine
immigrants were literate in English since the British had
established government schools in Ireland during the 1830s.
However, according to Patrick Blessing, the occupational
mobility, especially for Irish men, was one of the lowest
among immigrant groups during the nineteenth century (16).
They faced tremendous prejudice and discrimination until the
Civil War, and most Irish-Americans remained in ghetto-type
neighborhoods where they had their own social and fraternal
organizations, and of course, for the many Catholic Irish,
their own parishes.   Perhaps due to the combination of
their ability to speak and read English, and the
discrimination they faced, the Irish became very active in
politics. Beginning with Irish "bosses" in New York during
the nineteenth century and continuing up through Chicago's
Mayor Daley in the mid-twentieth century, Irish politicians
developed political machines which were envied and later
copied by members of other ethnic groups in many cities.
     The second significant factor in nineteenth century
Irish-American culture after the Famine was Ireland's
attempt to gain independence from Great Britain.   Irish
nationalism played an important role in the lives of many
Irish immigrants with a series of Irish-American and
Irish-Canadian organizations which began with the Society of
United Irishmen during the 1790s, continued with the Fenians
during the 1850s and 1860s, the Clan Na Gael in the
1860s-1880's, and continues with Irish northern aid groups
today.   One scholar even credits the Fenians with
contributing to Canada's independence from Great Britain due
to threats of Fenian invasions of Canada during the 1860s
(17). These groups held conferences, raised money, sent arms
and men to Ireland, and tried to influence events in both
Ireland and North America toward Irish independence.   A
considerable part of the most easily identified nineteenth
century material culture of the Irish relates to these
groups and to other fraternal and social organizations (18).
     At the same time, the Irish established a widespread
and significant religious system throughout the United
States through the Catholic Church that included schools,
churches, convents, seminaries, and hospitals.   These
institutions provide another potential source of
Irish-American material culture, although few have been
researched either from within or by outside scholars.   Those
that have provide an important look at Irish-American
culture through stained glass windows, statues, photographs,
and the buildings themselves.   Irish-American clergy also
played an important role in both Irish and American politics
as well as serving to create educational and social service
organizations for the Irish.
     Although it was never again as high as during the
Famine period (there were about 2.7 million immigrants to
the U.S. from 1851 to 1920), Irish immigration continued to
be significant through the turn of the century.   During the
second half of the 1800s, the majority of Irish who
emigrated were under thirty-five and unmarried. Unlike
several other ethnic groups, during most years of
immigration, as many women emigrated as men.   The women
tended to work as domestics or in factories, while the men
were usually laborers, soldiers, or in service jobs such as

bartending. Hasia Diner has pointed out that while Irish
men had difficulty achieving occupational mobility due to
the prejudice against them, Irish women were actually quite
successful in using domestic positions in particular to move
into mainstream American society. Educational opportunity
was provided to women through religious sponsored schools
established by orders of nuns including the Irish-based
Sisters of Mercy which in some cases exceeded that available
to Irish men (19). During this time, the Irish had migrated
to some extent away from the urban East Coast centers and
"by 1880, over one third of the Irish-born resided elsewhere
than on the East coast (20)."
    Perhaps because of the negative reaction to the massive
Irish immigration during the 1840's and 1850s, the Irish,
and especially their American-born children, quickly seemed
to become a part of the American mainstream. At the same
time, an Irish-American culture was established which had
its roots in the strong family ties of traditional Irish
society and according to some scholars, the Gaelic culture
of pre-English Ireland (21). Local Irish-American clubs
were established, as well as national organizations such as
the Ancient Order of Hibernians in America (1836), Catholic
Total Abstinence Union of America (1869), the Irish National
Land League of America (1880), and the Gaelic Athletic
Association (1890), some of which continue to the present.
Protestant Irish immigrants also established national groups
with the Loyal Orange Institution of the United States of
America in 1870 and the Scotch-Irish Society of America in
1889 (22). Irish newspapers, for example, the Irish
World in New York and the Boston Pilot, were also
established during this time and allowed information about
Ireland and Irish events in the United States to be
circulated in various Irish communities.
    The Irish had a tremendous impact on nineteenth and
twentieth century popular culture in music, vaudeville acts,
plays and literature. Famous Irish-American writers include
F. Scott Fitzgerald, John O'Hara, and James T. Farrell. By
the turn of the century, anti-Irish discrimination of the
virulent sort had disappeared and was replaced with the
affectionately stereotyped Mr. Dooley created by Finley
Peter Dunne, a humorist from Chicago who was popular from
the late 1800s to the early 1900s.
    The creation of the Irish Free State in 1921 (six
counties of Ulster were left under British rule) and the
establishment of the Irish Republic in 1949, affected both
immigration and the involvement of Irish-Americans with
Ireland. Immigration dropped during World War I, was up
again in 1920, dropped after the Depression, and remained
low until after World War II. The 1940s brought a steady
stream of Irish until the Immigration and Nationality Act of
1965. By 1972, 16.4 million Americans claimed Irish descent
to census takers.
    The massive influx of immigrants from other countries
to the United States from 1880-1930 put the Irish in a
position of control in many cities, especially those where
they had established strong Catholic parishes and political
machines. While their influence on politics and religion
has been researched heavily, the Irish influence on their

material surroundings has been little examined. The first
studies that really looked at Irish-American culture in this
century did not appear until the 1960s and 70s and most of
these concluded that the Irish have totally assimilated into
the American mainstream (23). In terms of occupations and
social status, this may be true, but Irish-American folklife
and popular culture have barely been examined, so we cannot
claim assimilation for something which has not yet been
studied. The interest in roots and cultural traditions
aroused during the 1970s has produced a number of
Irish-American societies and publications about
Irish-American activities. It is only very recently,
however, that the Irish and mainstream historical agencies
have begun to try to document Irish-American culture in any
systematic manner. Irish centers including museums and/or
archives have been established in San Francisco, Pittsburgh,
Chicago and New York (the last is in the planning stage).
This is in tremendous contrast to other ethnic groups such
as the Germans, Lithuanians, and Ukrainians who much earlier
created active ethnic museums, and to Italians, Poles,
Blacks, and Jews who have either established historical
institutions or have seen their cultural artifacts collected
by mainstream organizations.

The Irish in Canada have been even more neglected.
Since they are lumped into a general "British Isles"
category in most studies of Canadian ethnic groups, simple
demographic studies are difficult and identifying an Irish
Canadian material culture seems nearly impossible. However,
work by such groups as the Irish Canadian Cultural
Association of New Brunswick and scholarly studies such as
the excellent work done by John J. Mannion on Irish
Settlements in Eastern Canada show that there is
Irish-Canadian material culture which can be documented and
preserved (24).

Andrew Greeley has documented the American Irish in
several works and traced their movement from urban ghettos
to seeming assimilation in the suburbs. He notes:

> We may have become less aware of our
> Irishness in the process; we may have
> given up many of our memories and some
> of our skills. Some of us may even have
> tried to become good Wasp Americans; but
> at that we have failed. After three and
> four generations and lots of education and
> success, we remain incurably Irish...
> There is a distinctive Irish American
> subculture that has survived for a century
> without anyone paying much attention to it
> or even trying to keep it alive (25).

It is my hope that this volume will contribute to the work
of those who wish to document that subculture in its
material manifestations so that future generations of
Irish-Americans and Irish-Canadians will fully appreciate
the impact their ancestors had on the culture of North
America.

NOTES

1. Kerby Miller, Emigrants and Exiles: Ireland and
the Irish Exodus to North America (New York: Oxford
University Press, 1985), p. 11.

2. Ibid. p. 18. Miller gives a detailed and excellent
history of Ireland and Irish culture before and after
British conquest.

3. Patrick J. Blessing, "Irish," in Harvard
Encyclopedia of Ethnic Groups (Cambridge, Mass.: Harvard
University Press, 1980), p. 525.

4. Dennis Clark, Hibernia America: The Irish and
Regional Cultures (Westport, Conn.: Greenwood Press,
1986), p. 4.

5. Ibid. pp. 1-9.

6. Maldwyn A. Jones, "Scotch-Irish," in Harvard
Encyclopedia of Ethnic Groups, p. 900.

7. Desmond Fitz-gerald, "Irish Furniture and Its
Influence in Philadelphia 1720-1750," Program guide to
Philadelphia's Irish Legacy, 1984 Antiques Show,
Philadelphia: R. L. Raley, "Irish Influences in Baltimore
Decorative Arts 1785-1815," Antiques(March 1961): David
Stockwell, "Irish Influence in Pennsylvania Queen Anne
Furniture," Antiques (March 1961): Meric R. Rogers,
"Philadelphia via Dublin: Influences in Rococo Furniture,"
Antiques (March 1961).

8. Miller, Emigrants and Exiles, p. 164.

9. Ibid.

10. G. McWhiney and Forrest McDonald, "Celtic Names in
the Antebellum Southern United States," Names (1983):
89-102; F. McDonald and Ellen Shapiro McDonald, "The Ethnic
Origins of the American People, 1790," William and Mary
Quarterly (1980): 179-199; F. McDonald and G. McWhiney,
"The Celtic South," History Today, 30 (1980): 11-15.
Leroy Eid describes what he calls their Celtic Thesis in
detail and summarizes these and other articles.

11. Leroy V. Eid, "The Colonial Scotch-Irish: A View
Accepted Too Readily," Eire-Ireland (Winter 1986):
81-105. See Bibliography for traditional histories of
the Scotch-Irish.

12. Blessing, "Irish," p. 528.

13. Clark,Hibernia America, pp. 77-78.

14. See Dennis Clark, Hibernia America; Donald
Harman Akenson, Being Had, Historians, Evidence and the
Irish in North America, (P.D. Meany, Pub., 1985),
especially p. 70; and John Ridge, Erin's Sons in America,
The Ancient Order of Hibernians (New York: AOH

Publications, 1986).

15. Jones, "Scotch-Irish," p. 906.

16. Blessing, "Irish," pp. 529, 531.

17. W. S. Neidhart, <u>Fenianism in North America</u> (University Park: Penn State University Press, 1975).

18. <u>See</u> Michael Funchion, ed., <u>Irish American Voluntary Organizations</u> (Westport, Conn.: Greenwood Press, 1983) for an excellent summary of these and other Irish American groups.

19. Hasia Diner, <u>Erin's Daughters in America, Irish Immigrant Women in the 19th Century</u>, pp. 43-53, 121.

20. Blessing, "Irish," p. 530.

21. Miller,<u>Emigrants and Exiles</u>, p. 297. <u>Also</u> <u>see</u> Dennis Clark, "Folk Memory of the Urban Irish," <u>The New York Irish Newsletter</u>, 1986, pp. 11, 6.

22. Funchion,<u>Irish American Voluntary Organizations</u>, pp. 284-290.

23. <u>See for example</u> Lawrence J. McCaffrey, <u>The Irish Diaspora in America</u> (Bloomington: Indiana University Press, 1976), p. 181, and Andrew M. Greeley, <u>That Most Distressful Nation, The Taming of the American Irish</u> (Chicago: Quadrangle Books, 1972), p. 265.

24. John J. Mannion, <u>Irish Settlements in Eastern Canada, A Study of Cultural Transfer and Adaption</u> (Toronto: University of Toronto, Dept. of Geography, 1974).

25. Andrew Greeley, "The Irish," reprinted in <u>The Irish Directory</u>, ed. Frank Cull and John Concannon (New York: 1983), p. 2.

Irish American
Material Culture

CHAPTER I

Collections

SOURCES AND ARRANGEMENT

This chapter consists of descriptive entries of
repositories of Irish-American and Irish-Canadian material
culture. The data were compiled from current editions of
The Official Museum Directory, the Directory of
Historical Societies and Agencies in the United States and
Canada, other reference works listed in the bibliography,
and from the responses to questionnaires mailed to over 200
potential repositories during 1984-87.

The entries are arranged alphabetically by state or
province, then by municipality, then by name of institution.
Following the example of The Official Museum Directory,
Canadian entries follow United States entries.

SUGGESTIONS FOR RESEARCH

The researcher wishing to visit an institution should
always make an appointment, even if "No appointment
necessary" is indicated in the entries. Open hours may
be changed at short notice and the researcher may find the
repository closed. Furthermore, advance notice will give
the staff time to prepare registraral records for outside
use, retrieve special materials, etc.

It is further recommended that the researcher have at
least some knowledge of local or regional Irish-American
history before attempting research in visual resources. It
is always advisable to spend some time in the repository's
library or at a local historical society (in the case of
libraries and other non-historical organizations), before
examining the museum or photographic collections.

CA1   CALIFORNIA HISTORICAL SOCIETY
        Library

        2090 Pacific Avenue
        San Francisco, CA 94109
        (415) 567-1848

        Bruce L. Johnson, Library Director
        Staff: 8 permanent, 6 volunteer

        Collection not catalogued by ethnic group but
        includes 14 diaries from the Oliver family describing
        life in San Francisco in the 1840's and 50's. Also
        posters of the Woman's Irish Education League,
        Friends of Irish Freedom (1817), and the Irish
        Women's Mission. Posters, trade cards, broadsides,
        diaries. Photos: government, neighborhoods,
        occupations, people, politics and social movements,
        religion, structures, transportation.

        Dates: general collection covers 16th through 20th
        centuries.

        0% catalogued; library.

        Hours: W-Sat 1-5. No appointment necessary. Open
        to the public. $2.00 fee to non-members, $1.00 to
        students.

        Lends for special exhibits. Copies of photographs
        may be purchased for research and other
        non-commercial purposes. Reproduction and use fees
        charged. Schedule of fees and conditions for use
        available from Society.

                                +++++

CA2   UNITED IRISH CULTURE CENTER

        2700 45th Avenue
        San Francisco, CA 94116
        (415) 661-2700

        Patrick J. Dowling, Library Director
        Staff: 6 Library, 21 Institution

        Center includes a grand ballroom, restaurant, bar,
        meeting rooms and a library of over 5,000 volumes
        related to all things Irish, including a copy of the
        Book of Kells and a Gaelic Bible. Building was
        opened in 1975 and was built with labor and equipment
        donated by the Irish of San Francisco.
        Collection includes Ancient Order of Hibernian
        emblems, 1899-1984. Weapons, art objects
        (needlepoint hangings, paintings, busts), fraternal
        and social organization items, banners, flags, coins,
        stamps, piece of sod from Ireland, building, Irish

CA2   (United Irish Cultural Center)
cont.
        guest book. Photos: clubs and organizations, customs
        and celebrations, government, people, politics,
        sports, structures, Ireland.

        Library.

        Hours: W-Sat 1:30-4:30 and 7:30-9. No appointment
        necessary. Open to anyone interested in Ireland and
        its history. No research or admission fees.

        No loans.

                           +++++

CA3   SOCIETY OF CALIFORNIA PIONEERS

        456 McAllister Street
        San Francisco, CA   94947
        (415) 861-5278

        Grace Baker, Librarian
        Staff: 5 permanent

        Photos.

        Catalogued. Library.

        Hours: M-F 10-4. No appointment necessary.   Open to
        the public. No research or admission fees.

        No loans.

                           +++++

CO4   DENVER PUBLIC LIBRARY
        Western History Department

        1357 Broadway
        Denver, CO   80218
        (303) 571-2013

        Eleanor M. Gehres, Manager
        Staff: 12 permanent, 20-30 volunteer

        Collection not catalogued by Irish. Photos, oral
        history.

        Hours: M-W 10-9, T-Sat 10-5:30, Sun 1-5.
        No appointment necessary. Open to the public.
        No research or admission fees.

        No loans. Photographic procedures and fee schedule
        available.
                           +++++

                                        California-Colorado

CT5   CONNECTICUT HISTORICAL SOCIETY

        1 Elizabeth Street
        Hartford, CT 06105
        (203) 236-5621

        Everett Wilkie, Librarian
        Robert F. Trent, Curator
        Staff: 16 permanent, 30 volunteer

        Society mounted exhibit on the Irish in Connecticut
        in 1984. Also developed traveling exhibit and
        slide show on the Irish. Photos, objects.

        Not catalogued. Library.

        Hours: T-F 9-5 (Sept-May, Sat). No appointment
        necessary. Open to any qualifed researcher. $2.00
        fee for museum. No fee for library.

        Loans to appropriate institutions.

                                +++++

DE6   HAGLEY MUSEUM AND LIBRARY

        P.O. Box 3630
        Wilmington, DE   19807
        (302) 658-2400

        Maureen O'Brien Quimby, Curator
        Dan Muir, Photography
        Staff: 29 permanent, 80+ volunteer

        Museum has held Irish festival in past years.
        Many Irish immigrants were employed in the DuPont
        mills, and several of the restored buildings have
        ties to these workers and their families.
        Buildings, clothing, personal adornments,
        luggage, food processing and service articles,
        musical instruments, tools, broadsides.
        Photos: customs and celebrations, education, hotels,
        taverns, inns, household interiors, industry and
        commerce, occupations, people, religion, churches,
        structures.

        Library.

        Hours: M-F 8:30-4:30. Appointment necessary. Open
        to serious researchers and students. Fee to view
        collection, no fee for library.

        Loans. Fee for copy prints, restrictions on
        individual collections. Need to do prior research
        before using photo collection.

DE6   (Hagley Museum and Library)
cont.

       Cf. ELEUTHERIAN MILLS, DE96
           BRANDYWINE MANUFACTURERS' SUNDAY SCHOOL, DE95
           ST. JOSEPH'S ON THE BRANDYWINE, DE97

                              +++++

DE7   HISTORICAL SOCIETY OF DELAWARE

       505 Market Street Mall
       Wilmington, DE 19801
       (302) 655-7161

       Rebecca J. Hammell, Museum Curator
       Staff: 14 full-time, 2 part-time, 25 docents

       Collection includes a textile book by A. H. Rowan,
       Irish immigrant; and a lithograph by John Comerford
       of Ireland. Also George Read II house and gardens.
       Not catalogued by ethnic group. Photos. Building,
       personal adornments, textile sample, art objects.

       85% catalogued, 45% photographed. Library.

       Hours:_ Museum--T-F 12-4, Sat 10-4; Library T-F 9-5,
       M 1-9. Appointment needed for museum, not for
       library. Open to the public. No fees except for
       genealogical research.

       Loans under special circumstances.

                              +++++

DE8   WINTERTHUR MUSEUM LIBRARY

       Winterthur, DE 19735
       (302) 656-8591

       Dr. Frank H. Sommer, Head of Library
       Staff: 14 permanent, 20 volunteer.

       Collection includes membership certificate for
       Hibernian Society of Philadelphia (1796) drawn by
       John J. Barralet, Irish immigrant; and a
       hydrometer invented by Christopher Colles, also
       of Ireland. Art objects, tools, furniture. Oral
       history. Photos: advertisements, agriculture,
       animals, art, clothing, clubs and organizations,
       communication, criminals and crime, customs and
       celebrations, education, entertainment, foodways,
       government, hotels, taverns, inns, households,
       industry and commerce, health and medicine, military,
       music, nature, neighborhoods, occupations, people,
       politics, social movements, structures,
       transportation.

                                              Delaware

DE8   (Winterthur Museum Library)
cont.
        Dates: 1918-present.

        Catalogued. Library.

        Hours: M-F 8:30-4:30. No appointment necessary.
        Open to anyone with proper identification. Fee to
        view collections. No fee to use library.

        Loans for study and exhibition. Fee for copy prints.
        Some restrictions on photos.

                              +++++

DC9   THE CATHOLIC UNIVERSITY OF AMERICA LIBRARY
        Department of Archives and Manuscripts

        620 Michigan Avenue NE
        Washington, DC 20064
        (202) 635-5065

        Dr. Anthony Zito, Archivist
        Staff: 2 permanent

        Historical photographs, objects. Not catalogued.

        Hours: M-F 9-5. No appointment necessary. Open to
        the public. No research or admission fees.

        No loans.

                              +++++

DC10   SMITHSONIAN INSTITUTION
        Office of Folklife Programs Archive

        955 L'Enfant Plaza SW
        Room #2600
        Washington, DC 20560
        (202) 287-3251

        Pete Magoon, Archivist
        Staff: 2

        Collection of research and documentation related to
        the Festival of American Folklife, 1967-1987+.
        Photos, audio tapes, video tapes, motion picture
        film. Irish programs were included in the years
        1967, 1970, 1976, and 1985.

        Hours: M-F 9-5. Appointment necessary. Open to
        researchers. No admission or research fees.

                              +++++

                                          Delaware-Washington, DC

DC11   LIBRARY OF CONGRESS

        Washington, DC 20540
        (202) 287-5000

        *Prints and Photographs Division
        287-6394

        Mary Ison, Head Reference
        Staff: Very large

        Advertising media, broadsides. Photos: customs and
        celebrations, politics, entertainment, hotels,
        taverns, inns, people. Very large collection,
        some materials not catalogued or indexed.

        Hours: M-F 8:30-5. Appointment recommended. Open
        to the public. No fees.

        *Archive of Folk Culture
        287-5510

        Gerald E. Parsons, Reference Librarian
        Staff: 3 permanent, volunteer varies

        Hours: M-F 8:30-5. Appointment necessary for
        research listening. Open to the public. No fees.

        1979 Montana Folklife Survey collection includes
        music, dance, and story telling (Irish-American) in
        Montana.   Chicago Ethnic Arts Project Collection
        (1977) documented music, crafts, and customs of Irish
        in Chicago through sound recordings and photographs.
        Finding aids available. Also has broadsides and oral
        history. Photos: customs and celebrations,
        household interiors, home crafts, music, people.

        Music Division has an Irish-American popular music
        collection. Also materials in Geography and
        Map Division, Motion Picture, Rare Book, and Special
        Collections.

        Special arrangements can be made for loans. Contact
        Library of Congress Photoduplications Service for
        photocopies.

                            +++++

FL12   FLORIDA FOLKLIFE PROGRAM
        Archive

        P.O. Box 265
        White Springs, FL 32096
        (904) 397- 2192

        Ormond H. Loomis, Director
        Staff: 12 permanent

FL12   (Florida Folklife Program)
cont.

        Oral history. Not catalogued as Irish-American.
        Over 2,000 tapes.

        Hours: M-F 8-5. Appointment recommended. Open to
        the public. No research or admission fees.

        No loans.

                              +++++

IL13   ARCHDIOCESE OF CHICAGO
        Archives

        5150 Northwest Highway
        Chicago, IL 60630
        (312) 736-5150

        John J. Treanor, Assistant Chancellor for Archives
        Staff: 4 full time

        Photos. Collection is not currently catalogued by
        ethnic group. Prior research suggested.

        Hours: M-F 8-3:45. Appointment suggested. Open to
        the public. No research or admission fees.

        Loans for exhibits with proper arrangements.
        Fee for copy prints. Photocopying not encouraged.

                              +++++

IL14   CHICAGO HISTORICAL SOCIETY

        North Avenue and Clark Streets
        Chicago, IL 60614
        (312) 642-4600

        Larry Viskochil, Curator Graphics
        Susan Tillett, Director of Curatorial Affairs
        Staff: 110 permanent, volunteer varies

        Collection includes 1855 daguerrotype of Emmett
        Guards and Montgomery Guards; Michael "Hinky Dink"
        Kenna's beer schooner presented to the Women's
        Christian Temperance Union; ribbon from Irish Day at
        the Columbian Exposition. Clothing, weapons,
        furniture, art objects, political and fraternal
        items, ivory knife, diaries, religious objects,
        broadsides. Photos: customs and celebrations,
        military, people.

        Dates: 1700's to present, library.

                                        Florida-Illinois

IL14   (Chicago Historical Society)
cont.
        Hours: T-Sat 9:30-4:30. Appointment suggested.
        Open for research to anyone high school age and up.
        No research fees, fee to view exhibits.

        Loans for exhibits. Copy fees.

                              +++++

IL15   CHICAGO PUBLIC LIBRARY
        Special Collections

        78 East Washington Street
        Chicago, IL 60602
        (312) 269-2926

        Richard Kaplan
        Staff: 4 permanent, volunteer varies

        Collection includes religious objects, broadsides,
        fraternal and social organization items. Photos:
        clubs and organizations, neighborhoods, occupations,
        people, politics, structures.

        Dates: Photos--1860's-present.

        25% catalogued.

        Hours: M-F 12-4. No appointment necessary. Open to
        the public. No fees for using library.

        Loans for exhibits only. Fee for copy prints, must
        credit Chicago Public Library on copies.

                              +++++

IL16   IRISH AMERICAN HERITAGE CENTER

        4626 North Knox Ave
        Chicago, IL 60630
        (312) 282-7035

        Mary O'Reilly, Board Member
        Staff: 1 permanent, 200 volunteer.

        The Center is currently being renovated. When
        completed it will include a museum, library, theater,
        and meeting rooms. A number of local Irish
        organizations currently use the center. Collections
        include needlework piece by Lily Yeats, Irish
        cultural maps including Ireland's contributions to
        Europe and a Chicago Irish Folklife Map. Also has
        the organ from St. Patrick's Church in St. Charles.
        Musical instruments, pottery, art objects, fraternal
        and social organization items. Photos: customs and

IL16   (Irish American Heritage Center)
cont.

        celebrations, entertainment, people, politics.
        Cultural Display of the Irish Literary Tradition and
        Washington's Irish.

        Library.

        Hours: M-F 9-5. Appointment necessary. Open to the
        public. No research or admission fees.

        No loans. Collection is in storage.

                         +++++

IL17   LOYOLA UNIVERSITY OF CHICAGO
        University Archives

        6525 Sheridan
        Chicago, Il 60626
        (312) 274-3000

        University Archivist
        Staff: 2 permanent, 3 part-time

        Library has large collection of books on Ireland
        from the 1920's. University was mostly Irish before
        WWII. Photos. Prior research suggested.

        Library.

        Hours: M-F 8:45-11:45, 1:15-4:45. Please call for
        appointment. No research or admission fees.

        Loans for special exhibits.

                         +++++

IL18   SISTERS OF MERCY PROVINCE CENTER
        Archives

        1024 Central Park
        Chicago, IL 60642
        (312) 776-0248

        Sister Mary Noreen, Archivist
        Staff: 1 permanent

        The Sisters of Mercy Order was founded in Dublin
        and has included many Irish immigrants in its work
        in the United States. Photos: clothing, people,
        education, structures, interiors. Religious objects,
        art objects, postcards.

        Hours: M-Th 8-12. Appointment necessary. Serious
        researchers. No admission or research fees.

                                               Illinois

IL18   (Sisters of Mercy Province Center)
cont.

        Only loans for Mercy-sponsored exhibits.   Fee for
        copy prints.

                        +++++

IL19   UNIVERSITY OF ILLINOIS AT CHICAGO

        Halsted and Harrison Streets
        Chicago, IL   60680

        *Jane Addams Hull House Museum
        P.O. Box 4348
        (312) 996-2793

        Mary Ann Johnson, Director, Hull House
        Staff: 3 permanent, 3 volunteer

        Museum on National Register of Historic Places-
        contains permanent and rotating exhibits including
        to the life of Jane Addams, the work of Hull House,
        and its relationship to the surrounding neighborhood,
        a substantial portion of which was Irish at one time.
        Permanent exhibit on ethnic groups in the Hull House
        neighborhood as well as a slide tape program on the
        Irish in Chicago.   Structures, luggage, art objects,
        broadsides, diaries.   Photos.

        Hours: M-F 10-4, Sun 12-5.   Appointment recommended.
        No research or admission fees.

        No loans.

        *Manuscripts Department
        Library
        P.O. Box 8198
        996-2742

        Mary Ann Bamberger, Head
        Staff: 8 Special Collections

        Jane Addams Memorial Collection photographs include
        residents of near west side of Chicago.   Photos from
        A Century of Progress including the Irish-American
        Village.   Photos: people, neighborhoods, customs and
        celebrations.

        Hours: M-F 8:30-4:30.   No appointment necessary.
        Open to researchers.   No admission or research fees.

                        +++++

IL20   WEST CHICAGO HISTORICAL MUSEUM

        132 Main Street
        Department C
        West Chicago IL   60185
        (312) 231-3376

        Luann Bombard, Director
        Staff: 2 permanent, part-time

        During the 1840's-1870's the majority of West
        Chicago's foreign-born residents were Irish who came
        to work on the railroad. While objects are not
        catalogued by ethnic group, it is likely that much
        of the museum's collection has ties to the Irish
        population. Museum is especially strong in railroad
        material.

        Photos: taverns, occupations, people, transportation,
        industry and commerce.

        Library.

        Hours: Th-Sat 10-3 or by appointment. Appointment
        necessary. Open to the public. No fees for
        research.

        Loans for exhibits.

                          +++++

IN21   INDIANA STATE MUSEUM

        202 North Alabama Street
        Indianopolis, IN   46204
        (317) 232-1637

        Linda Badger, Assistant Registrar
        Staff: 70+ permanent

        Collection contains a Clark Irish Harp made in
        Syracuse, NY 1910-1920. Musical instruments.

        Library.

        Hours: M-F 8-4:30. Appointment necessary. Open to
        the public with permission. No fees for research.

        Loans for exhibits.

                          +++++

IA22   NEW MELLERAY ABBEY

        RR 1
        Dubuque, IA 52001
        (319) 588-2319

IA22   (New Melleray Abbey)
cont.

        Fr. Pius Hanley, Gift Shop

        The abbey was founded by Irish monks from Mt.
        Melleray in County Waterford, Ireland, in 1849.

        Several of the nearby towns and settlements in
        this part of Iowa were founded by Irish immigrants.
        Collection includes a statue from Ireland brought
        in 1849. Buildings, religious objects.

        Hours: M-F 9-11:30, 2-5. Appointment necessary.

                              +++++

KS23   KANSAS STATE HISTORICAL SOCIETY
        Center for Historical Research

        120 West 10th Street
        Topeka, KS 66612
        (913) 296-3165

        Nancy Sherbert, Curator of Photographs
        Staff: 4 permanent, 1 volunteer

        Collection is not catalogued by Irish. Photos.
        Currently being cataloged on computer.

        Dates: 1854-present

        Library.

        Hours: M-F 9-5 Sat 8-12. No appointment necessary.
        Open to the public. No admission or research fees.

        Loans sometimes. Copy fee.

                              +++++

LA24   HISTORIC NEW ORLEANS COLLECTION

        533 Royal Street
        New Orleans, LA 70130
        (504) 523-4662

        Dode Platou, Chief Curator
        Pamela D. Arceneaux, Reference Librarian
        Staff: 60 permanent, volunteer varies

        Advertising media, broadsides, art objects, fraternal
        and social organization items, diaries. Photos:
        advertisements, agriculture, animals, art,
        clothing, clubs and organizations, communication,
        criminals and crime, customs and celebrations,
        disasters, education, entertainment, foodways,

LA24   (Historic New Orleans Collection)
cont.
        fishing and hunting, government, hotels, taverns,
        inns, household, industry and commerce, health and
        medicine, military, music, nature, neighborhoods,
        occupations, people, politics, social movements,
        structures, transportation. (Not indexed by Irish)

        Dates: photos--1840's-present

        Catalogued. Library.

        Hours: T-Sat 10-4:30. Appointment preferred. Open
        to the public. No admission or research fees.

        No loans except for exhibits.
        Fee for copy prints, restrictions on use of photos.

                              +++++

MD25   MUSEUM AND LIBRARY OF MARYLAND HISTORY
        The Maryland Historical Society

        201 West Monument Street
        Baltimore, MD 21201
        (301) 685-3750

        Staff: 48 full-time, 21 part-time. 463 volunteer.

        Has papers of Associated Friends of Ireland in the
        City of Baltimore 1828-1835. Also Hibernian Society
        Papers (1816-1978), which include memorabilia and
        scrapbooks. Food processing and service articles.
        Collection is not indexed by ethnic group,
        so prior research is necessary.

        Library.

        Hours: T-F 11-4:30, Sat 9-4:30. Appointment
        necessary. Anyone may use collection. Fee to view
        collections and library.

        Loans for exhibits. Fee charged for copies used for
        publication. $12-27.

                              +++++

MD26   BALTIMORE CITY LIFE MUSEUMS
        Museum Reference Center

        800 East Lombard Street   Mail to:
        Baltimore, MD 21202   225 Holliday Street
        (301) 396-1149   Baltimore, MD 21202

        Dean Krimmel, Supervisor
        Staff: 3 permanent, 2 volunteer.

                                          Louisiana-Maryland

MD26   (Baltimore City Life Museums)
cont.
        Baltimore City Life Museums include the Peale Museum,
        the Carroll Mansion, the Center for Urban
        Archaeology, the H. L. Mencken House, and the 1840
        House. Collections include advertising media,
        broadsides, fraternal and social organization items.
        Photos: advertisements, customs and celebrations,
        hotels, taverns, inns; politics; religious.

        Dates: Late 19th century-present.

        100% Catalogued. Library.

        Hours: W-F 10-4:30. Appointment encouraged. Open
        to the public. No admission or research fees.

        Loans only to institutions. Write for photo-
        duplication service conditions and charges.

        Cf. CARROLL MANSION, MD105

                            +++++

MA27   BOSTON ATHENAEUM

        10 1/2 Beacon Street
        Boston, MA 02108
        (617) 227-0270

        Sally Pierce, Curator of Prints and Photographs
        Staff: 44 permanent, 1-3 volunteer

        Historic photographs. (May have oral history.) Not
        catalogued by ethnic group. Must know specific
        individuals, neighborhood, street address, etc.

        Partially catalogued. Library.

        Hours: M-F 9-5:30, Sat 9-4 (Oct-May). Appointment
        strongly recommended for prints and photos
        department. No admission or research fees.

        Loans for exhibits.

                            +++++

MA28   BOSTON PUBLIC LIBRARY
        Print Department

        666 Boylston Street
        Copley Square
        Boston, MA 02117
        (617) 536-5400 ext. 280

        Keeper of Prints
        Staff: 4 permanent

MA28   (Boston Public Library)
cont.
       Large photograph collection including Boston
       Political Archive, The Boston Irish, and Round Towers
       by Hills. Also art depicting churches, religious
       themes, and structures. Art objects, advertisements.

       Photos: occupations, people, politics, social
       movements, temperance.

       Dates: 1856-1970.

       Not catalogued. Library.

       Hours: M-F 9-5. Appointment necessary to do
       research. Open to the public. No admission or
       research fees.

       Loans for special exhibits only. Copies of
       photographs may be purchased.

                          +++++

MA29   THE BOSTONIAN SOCIETY

       Old State House
       206 Washington Street
       Boston, MA   02109
       (617) 242-5614

       Philip Bergen, Librarian
       Tommy Parker, Director
       Staff: 12 permanent, 4 volunteer

       Society is Boston City Historical Society.
       Collections include structures, bedding, furniture,
       lighting devices, clothing, personal adornments,
       luggage, toilet articles, weapons, food processing
       and service articles, housekeeping tools, musical
       instruments, clocks, pottery, transportation,
       advertising media, religious objects, broadsides,
       art objects, games, toys and dolls, fraternal and
       social items, containers, diaries. Prints and slides
       of most objects available. Photos: advertisements,
       art, clothing, clubs and organizations, customs and
       celebrations, disasters, education, entertainment,
       foodways, hotels, taverns, inns, household, home
       crafts, industry and commerce, health and medicine,
       military, music, nature, neighborhoods, occupations,
       people, politics, structures, transportation, marine,
       and Old State House.

       Catalogued. Library.

       Hours: Library M-F 9:30-4:30. Appointment
       recommended. Open to the public. No research fees.
       Fee to view collections--$1.25 adults, $0.75
       children.
                                    Massachusetts

MA29   (The Bostonian Society)
cont.

        Loans for exhibits. Some restrictions on photos.
        Fee for copy prints, $12 for 8x10.

                            +++++

MA30   MASSACHUSETTS HISTORICAL SOCIETY

        1154 Boylston St.
        Boston, MA   02215
        (617) 536-1608

        Peter Drummey, Associate Librarian
        Staff: 24 permanent, several volunteer

        Manuscript repository and research library.
        Very small collection of Irish-related objects and
        photos. Has records of the Charitable Irish Society.
        Historical photos, objects.

        100% catalogued. Library.

        Hours: M-F 9-4:45. Appointment suggested.
        Open to serious researchers. No admission or
        research fees.

        Loans for exhibit only. No fees except for copying.

                            +++++

MA31   MUSEUM OF FINE ARTS
        American Decorative Arts Department

        465 Huntington Avenue
        Boston, MA   02115
        (617) 267-9300

        Jennifer Dragone, NMA intern
        Staff: large

        Saturday Evening Girls pottery decorated by Irish
        immigrants. Pottery.

        Library.

        Hours: Museum T, Th-Sun 10-5, W 10-10. Must have
        appointment. Fee to view collection, no fee to use
        library.

        Loans.

                            +++++

MA32   SOCIETY FOR THE PRESERVATION OF NEW ENGLAND
        ANTIQUITIES
        Harrison Gray Otis House

        141 Cambridge Street
        Boston, MA 02114
        (617) 227-3956

        Ellie Reichlin, Archivist
        Staff: 2 permanent

        Rich collection of photographs of South Boston and
        Dorcester. Prior research strongly suggested as
        photographs are not catalogued by ethnic group.
        Photos: advertisements, agriculture, animals, art,
        clothing, clubs and organizations, customs and
        celebrations, disasters, education, entertainment,
        foodways, fishing, hunting and trapping, hotels,
        taverns, inns, household, home crafts, industry and
        commerce, health and medicine, military, music,
        neighborhoods, occupations, people, structures,
        transportation.

        Dates: 1840's-present.

        Hours: M-F 9:30-5:00. By appointment only. Open to
        the public. No research or admission fees.

        Loans for exhibits.

                            +++++

MA33   ARCHDIOCESE OF BOSTON
        Archives

        2121 Commonwealth Avenue
        Brighton, MA   02135
        (617) 254-0100 ext. 142

        Timothy Meagher, Archivist
        Staff: 3 permanent

        Collection includes structures, clothing, personal
        adornments, religious objects, art objects, fraternal
        and social organization items, diaries. Photos:
        clubs and organizations, customs and celebrations,
        education, music, neighborhoods, people, politics,
        structures, religious. Collection is indexed but
        not by ethnic group.

        Dates: 1789-1986.

        Hours: M-F 9-4:45. No appointment necessary.
        Open to the public. No admission or research fees.

        No loans. Copy prints $10.

                            +++++
                                        Massachusetts

MA34   BOSTON COLLEGE
        Burns Library

        Chestnut Hill, MA   02167
        (617) 552-4861

        John Atteberry, Acting Reference Librarian
        Staff: 5 permanent, 2 volunteer

        Irish artifacts ancillary to over 6,000 volumes on
        Ireland. Collection includes stained glass windows
        with Irish themes by Richard King, statue of Our Lady
        of Knock, Hibernian regalia. Also a number of
        paintings by Irish artists. Pottery (glass),
        religious objects, broadsides, art objects, fraternal
        and social organization items.

        Hours: M-F 9-5. Appointment strongly recommended.
        Scholars, serious students, and researchers may use
        library. No admission or research fees. Collections
        are closed except for items currently on exhibit.

        Loans to institutions.

                            +++++

MA35   ANCIENT ORDER OF HIBERNIANS DIVISION 8

        408 Appleton Street
        Lawrence, MA 01840
        (717) 687-8937

        David Burke

        Private collection of Ancient Order of Hibernian
        memorabilia and photos. Fraternal and social
        organization items including a 1925 Ancient Order of
        Hibernians convention cup. Photos: people.

        Dates: early 1900's-present.

        Hours: by appointment only. Serious researchers
        only.
                            +++++

MA36   IMMIGRANT CITY ARCHIVES

        135 Parker Street
        Lawrence, MA 01810
        (617) 686-9230

        Eartha Dengler, Director
        Staff: 2 permanent, 10 volunteer

        Organization interested in multi-ethnic history
        studies. Very interested in collecting ethnic

MA36   (Immigrant City Archives)
cont.
         materials. Collection includes advertising media,
         diaries. Photos: advertisements, clubs and
         organizations, customs and celebrations, disasters,
         education, hotels, taverns, inns, industry and
         commerce, neighborhoods, people, politics,
         structures, transportation. Oral history.

         Dates: Photos-1845- present. Oral History 100%
         catalogued. Library.

         Hours: T, Th, F 9-5. Appointment necessary.
         Open to adults, serious researchers. No admission or
         research fees.

         Loans only in some cases. Fees for copy prints,
         restrictions on photo use.

                          .   +++++

MA37   MUSEUM OF AMERICAN TEXTILE HISTORY

         800 Massachusetts Avenue
         North Andover, MA 01845
         (617) 686-0191

         Marion Hall, Collections Secretary
         Staff: 25 permanent, 4 volunteer

         Collection includes spinning wheels, textile tools.
         Photos: occupations, structures.

         Dates: Photos: 1840-1950. Library.

         Hours: M-F 9-5. Appointment necessary. Open to
         adults. No admission or research fees.

         Loans for exhibits. $10 fee for copy prints.

                                     +++++

MA38   COLLEGE OF THE HOLY CROSS
         Dinand Memorial Library

         Worcester, MA 01610
         (617) 793-2506

         James Hogan, Director
         Staff: 25-30 professional, 60 student

         The Richard O'Flynn Collection includes numerous
         records of Irish societies, churches, cemetaries,
         military groups (Jackson and Emmet Guards) and
         letters from the 1860's. Also has Civil war
         furlough certificates from the Jackson Guards. Art

MA38   (College of the Holy Cross)
cont.
         objects. Photos: clubs and organizations, military,
         people, structures (churches). Oral history.

         Dates: 1850-1905.

         Hours: M-Sun 8:30-1 AM, F-Sat-11 AM. Summer M-F
         9-5. Appointment necessary. Open to the public. No
         admission or research fees.

         Loans for exhibits.

                              +++++

MA39   WORCESTER HISTORICAL MUSEUM

         39 Salisbury Street
         Worcester, MA   01603
         (617) 753-8278

         Mark Savolis, Curator of Manuscripts
         Rick Riccio, Curator
         Staff: 8 permanent

         Collection includes advertising media, fraternal and
         social organization items, pamphlet material.
         Photos: advertisements, clubs and organizations,
         industry and commerce, occupations, and people.

         Dates: Photos--1850-present. Library.

         Hours: T-Sat 10-4. No appointment necessary. Open
         to the public. No research or admission fees.

         Loans for special exhibits. $20 copy fee for prints.
         Restrictions on use of photos.

                              +++++

MI40   DETROIT INSTITUTE OF ARTS

         5200 Woodward Avenue
         Detroit, MI   48202
         (313) 833-7900

         Pamela Watson, Assistant Registrar
         or specific curatorial department
         Staff: 150 permanent, volunteer varies

         Large number of drawings, prints, and paintings by
         Irish and Irish-American artists. Collection
         includes painting of McSorley's Bar (Ale House) in
         New York City done in 1912 by John Sloan. Objects
         from Ireland include a wooden staircase from
         Eyrecourt Castle in Galway, made in the late 17th

MI40   (Detroit Institute of Arts)
cont.
        century, and British coins from 1251 and 1509.
        Furniture, pottery, silver, art objects, fraternal
        and social organization items, containers, coins.
        Photographs: art, hotels, taverns, inns; interiors.
        Fine Arts Collection is catalogued on computer as
        Detroit Art Registration and Information System
        (DARIS) and is computer-linked with 13 other
        Michigan museums. Library.

        Hours: M-F 9-4:30. (Museum closed on M).
        Appointment necessary. Open to students and serious
        researchers. No admission or research fees.

        Loans with some restrictions. Photocopying
        available.

                          +++++

MI41   DETROIT PUBLIC LIBRARY
        Burton Historical Collection

        5201 Woodward
        Detroit, MI 48202
        (313) 833-1480

        Alice Dalligan, Chief
        Staff: 12 permanent

        Historical photographs. Integrated into collection.
        Prior research necessary.

        Hours: M-F 9:30-5:30, W 9-9. No appointment
        necessary. Open to the public. No research or
        admission fees.

        No loans.

                          +++++

MI42   APPEL, JOHN AND SELMA

        219 Oakland Drive
        East Lansing, MI 48823
        (517) 337-1859

        John and Selma Appel
        Staff: 2 permanent

        The Appels' collection includes over 400 slides and
        over 400 original cartoons/caricatures relating to
        Irish-American stereotypes. Collection includes
        postcards, magazine cartoons, sheet music, posters,
        labels, and actors' make-up manuals. Advertising
        media, toys, and dolls. Photos: slides of advertise-
        ments, cartoons.

                                             Michigan

MI42   (Appel, John and Selma)
cont.
          In process of cataloging.

          Hours: By appointment only. Academic researchers
          may use collection with advance permission. No
          research or admission fees.

          Loans for exhibits. Will do research for publishers
          and institutions for fee.

                              +++++

MN43   UNIVERSITY OF MINNESOTA-MORRIS
          West Central Minnesota Historical Center

          Morris, MN 56267
          (612) 589-2211

          Staff: 1 permanent, 2 volunteer

          Tapes of the Irish-American community of Clontarf.
          Also school records, store and club records, and
          local histories. Oral history, maps.

          Dates: late 1800's-1979.

          Catalogued. Library.

          Hours: M and W 1-5, T and Th 2-5, F 10-12, 1-3. No
          appointment necessary. Open to the public. No
          research or admission fees.

          No loans.

                              +++++

MN44   HISTORIC MURPHY'S LANDING

          2187 Highway 101
          Shakopee, MN 55379
          (612) 445-6900

          Mariann Reid, Program Manager
          Staff: 2 permanent, 40 volunteer

          A living history museum of 1840-1890. Restored
          buildings include the O'Connor House, built by an
          Irish immigrant in Shakopee in 1865. Photos,
          objects, building.

          Hours: M-F 9-4. Appointment necessary. Open to the
          public. Fee to view museum.

          No loans.

                              +++++

MN45   MINNESOTA HISTORICAL SOCIETY

       *Museum Collections Department
       1500 Mississippi Street
       St. Paul, MN 55101
       (612) 296-0147

       Hilary Toven, Museum Collections Assistant
       Staff: 5 permanent, 2 volunteer

       Portrait collection includes over 100 photos with
       Irish-American connections. Also have bedding,
       clothing, personal adornments, luggage, toilet
       articles, textile tools, woodworking/other tools,
       fraternal and social organization buttons,
       containers, smoking pipes. Oral history. Photos:
       people.

       Dates: 1840's-present.

       80% catalogued; 30% photographed; library.

       Hours: M-F 8:30-5:00. Appointment necessary for
       research with collections. Open to serious
       researchers. No admission or research fees.

       Museum loans for exhibits. Copy prints $3.50, slides
       $1.50.

       *Reference Library
       690 Cedar Street
       St. Paul, MN 55706
       (612) 296-2143

       Patricia Harpole, Chief Librarian
       Staff: 15 permanent, 3 volunteer

       Dates: 1850's-present.

       100% catalogued.

       Hours: M-Sat 8:30-5:00. No appointment necessary.
       Open to the public. No admission or research fees.

       Rarely loans.

                          +++++

MO46   MISSOURI HISTORICAL SOCIETY

       Lindell and DeBaliviere   Mail to:
       Streets   Jefferson Memorial
       St. Louis, MO   Building
       (314) 361-1424   Forest Park
                                      St. Louis, MO 63112

       Duane Sneddeker, Curator of Photographs
       Staff: 43
                                      Minnesota-Missouri

MO46   (Missouri Historical Society)
cont.
        Photos, art objects.

        Not catalogued by ethnic group. Library.

        Hours: M-F 9:30-4:45. Appointment necessary to do
        research. Open to qualifed researchers and students.
        Fee to use library and collections.

        Loans considered upon written application to
        appropriate curator.

                        +++++

NE47   NEBRASKA STATE HISTORICAL SOCIETY

        1500 R Street
        Lincoln, NE 68501
        (402) 471-3270

        Gail Potter, Curator of Collections
        Staff: 100 permanent, 200 volunteer

        Archives has Murphy family collection. Bedding
        (quilt), clothing, weapons, clock, woodworking
        tools, broadsides, shillelagh.

        Hours: M-Sat 8-5, Sun 1:30-5. Appointment necessary
        to do research with collections. Open to the public.
        No research or admission fees.

        Loans to qualified institutions.

                        +++++

NE48   UNION PACIFIC RAILROAD MUSEUM

        1416 Dodge Street
        Omaha, NE 68179
        (402) 271-3530

        Don Snoddy, Curator
        Staff: 1 permanent

        Historical photographs. Prior research necessary.

        Catalogued. (Not by ethnic group). Library.

        Hours: M-F 9-5. Appointment necessary. Open to the
        public. No admission or research fees.

        Loans sometimes.

                        +++++

NV49   NEVADA HISTORICAL SOCIETY

       1650 North Virginia Street
       Reno, NV 89503-1799
       (702) 789-0190

       Miss Lee Mortenson, Research Librarian
       Staff: 8 permanent, 6 volunteer

       No specific material collection but Territorial
       Enterprise Newspaper has been indexed through 1881
       and includes information on the Ancient Order of
       Hibernians, Fenian Brotherhood, Irish Confederation,
       Knights of the Red Branch, Irish-American Benevolent
       Society, Irish American Brass Band, Irish Land
       League, Irish Union Club, and the Irishmen of Gold
       Hill.

       Newspaper index. Library.

       Hours: W-Sun 10-5. Appointment suggested. Open to
       the public. No research or admission fees.

       No loans.

                          +++++

NJ50   CAMDEN COUNTY HISTORICAL SOCIETY

       Park Boulevard and Euclid Avenue
       Camden, NJ 08103
       (609) 964-3333

       Margaret H. Weatherly, Director
       Staff: 8 permanent, 40 volunteer

       Exhibits and Irish Festival in 1985. Collection
       includes objects, oral history. Published The Irish
       in Camden County, by Joseph Kelly, in 1984.

       Library.

       Hours: M-Th 12:30-4:30, Sun 2-4:30.

                          +++++

NJ51   HISTORICAL SOCIETY OF PRINCETON

       158 Nassau Street
       Princeton, NJ 080542
       (609) 921-6748

       Ann Johanson, Librarian
       Staff: 2 full-time, 4 part-time.

       Historical photos.

NJ51   (Historical Society of Princeton)
cont.
        Not catalogued by ethnic group. Library.
        Hours: Library:T-F 10-4, Museum: T&F and Sat&Sun
        12-4. No appointment necessary. Open to the public.
        No admission or research fees.

        Loans for exhibits.

                          +++++

NY52   ANCIENT ORDER OF HIBERNIANS
        Division 5

        91 Quail Street
        Albany, NY 12206
        (518) 489-3144

        Mike Hession
        Staff: 1 volunteer

        Historical photographs. Private Collection.

        Hours: Evenings only. Must have appointment. No
        research or admission fees.

                          +++++

NY53   THE COLLEGE OF ST. ROSE

        432 Western Avenue
        Albany, NY 12203
        (518) 454-5111

        Catherine Cavanaugh, Curator
        Staff: all   volunteer

        The College of St. Rose is the current home of the
        projected New York Irish Museum. Artifacts and
        materials are still being collected.

        Library.

        Hours not set yet. Open to the public. No admission
        or research fees.

        Materials do not circulate.

                          +++++

NY54   CHEMUNG COUNTY HISTORICAL SOCIETY

        415 East Water Street
        Elmira, NY 14901
        (607) 734-4167

NY54   (Chemung County Historical Society)
cont.
          Timothy L. Decker, Curator of Collections
          Staff: 5 permanent, 30 volunteer

          Collection includes historical photographs and
          objects. Museum sponsored Irish Night in March
          1986.

          Collection catalogued, but not by ethnicity.
          Library.

          Hours: Museum: T-F 12-5, Sat 1-4, Office: M-F 9-5.
          Appointment preferred. Open to serious researchers.
          Fees for library/collection, $5 to non-members,
          $10 for mail inquiries.

          Loans for exhibits.

                              +++++

NY54A   IRISH AMERICAN CULTURAL CENTER OF NEW YORK

          33-71 164th Street
          Flushing, NY   11358
          (718) 939-1084

          John Concannon, Curator
          Staff: 1 permanent, 1 volunteer

          The Irish American Cultural Center is currently
          being organized. Its collection will include
          objects, photographs, and oral history related to
          the Irish in the New York metropolitan area.

          Not catalogued.

          Hours not set yet. Appointment necessary. Open to
          legitimate researchers. No admission or research
          fees.

          Will loan for exhibits.

                              +++++

NY55   AMERICAN IRISH HISTORICAL SOCIETY

          991 Fifth Avenue
          New York, NY   10028
          (212) 288-2263

          Thomas M. Bayne, Director
          Staff: 2 permanent, 3 volunteer

          The building housing the society was donated to the
          AIHS in 1940 by the Irish Palace Building
          Association. Its five floors include numerous

NY55   (American Irish Historical Society)
cont.

        paintings and photographs of Irish-Americans and
        Irish including Robert Emmet and Daniel
        O'Connell. Library houses over 15,000 volumes
        relating to Irish and Irish-American subjects.
        Structures, furniture, personal adornments,
        shillelaghs, musical instruments, clocks, pottery,
        religious objects, art objects, fraternal and social
        items, busts. Photos: people, politics, military,
        music.

        Collection not catalogued. Library.

        Hours: T-Sat 10-5. Appointment necessary. Open to
        members of society, researchers. No research or
        admission fees.

        No loans.
                            +++++

NY56   AMERICAN MUSEUM OF IMMIGRATION

        Liberty Island
        New York, NY 10004
        (212) 732-1236

        Paul Kinney, Curator
        Staff: 6 permanent, 1 volunteer

        About 5% of collection related to Irish-Americans.
        Also have an immigrant's letter to a friend,
        naturalization certificate, and sheet music.
        Personal adornments, pottery, religious objects,
        art objects, containers, 1 bag of sod, passport,
        oral history. Photographs: people.

        Dates: 1800-present. 75% catalogued, 100%
        photographed. Library.

        Hours: 9:30-5. Appointment required. Open to the
        public. Fees for ferryboat, no admission or research
        fees.

        Loans to institutions only. Photo collection not
        indexed, $10 copy print fee for black and white,
        $3 fee for slides.

                            +++++

NY57   BETTMAN ARCHIVE

        136 East 57th Street
        New York, NY 10022
        (212) 758-0362

        Staff: 50 permanent

NY57   (Bettman Archive)
cont.
         Collection not indexed by ethnic group. Photos.

         Hours: M-F 9-5. Must have appointment. Open to
         communications professionals. Fee to use collection.

         No loans. Fee for copy prints.

                          +++++

NY58   METROPOLITAN MUSEUM OF ART
         American Wing

         Fifth Avenue at 82nd Street
         New York, NY 10028
         (212) 879-5500

         Peter Kenny, Installation Coordinator
         Staff: 26 permanent, 12-15 volunteer

         Collection includes a side table by Irish-American
         furniture maker Joseph B. Barry, and several silver
         pieces by Irish-America silversmith Philip Syng.
         Furniture, silver.

         100% catalogued; 100% photographed. Library.

         Hours: T-Sun 9-5:30. Appointment necessary. Open
         to the public by appointment. No research or
         admission fees.

         Loans for exhibits.

                          +++++

NY59   MUSEUM OF THE CITY OF NEW YORK

         5th Avenue at 103rd Street
         New York, NY 10029
         (212) 534-1672

         Print Department, Decorative Arts Department
         Staff: 72 permanent, 25 volunteer

         Historical photographs. May have objects but no
         information is available.

         80% catalogued; 10% photographed. No library.

         Hours: T-Sat 10-5, Sun 1-5. Appointment necessary.
         Open to public. No research or admission fees.

         Loans for exhibits.

                          +++++

NY60   NEW YORK CITY FIRE MUSEUM

        278 Spring Street
        New York, NY 10013
        (212) 691-1303

        Jim Selby, Director
        Staff: 2

        This is a new museum which has the combined
        collections of the New York City Fire Department
        and the Home Insurance Company. Collection is being
        catalogued but contains historical photographs,
        art objects, and other objects related to the
        history of fire fighting in New York. There has
        been a long connection between the Irish of New
        York and the Fire Department, and many objects and
        photographs will have Irish ties. Prior research
        suggested. Photos: occupations, people, disasters.

        Not catalogued. Small library.

        Hours: T-Sat 10-4. Appointment necessary. Open to
        the public. No admission or research fees, but
        a donation is suggested.

        No loans.

                            +++++

NY61   NEW YORK HISTORICAL SOCIETY
        Print Department

        170 Central Park West
        New York, NY 10024
        (212) 873-3400

        Wendy Shadwell, Curator of Prints
        Staff: 2 permanent

        Society sponsored exhibit in 1984 on The Irish and
        Irish Organizations in New York City before 1900.
        Broadsides, diaries (in library). Photos: clubs and
        organizations, customs and celebrations, military,
        immigration. Other departments may have materials.

        Library. Some materials listed under Irish.

        Hours: Winter T-Sat 10-5; Summer M-F 10-5.
        Appointment necessary for some collections. Open to
        the public.

        Loans to qualified institutions. Schedule of copy
        fees available.

                            +++++

                                          New York

NY62   NEW YORK PUBLIC LIBRARY

        5th Avenue and 42nd Street
        New York, NY 10018
        (212) 930-0818

        Prints and Photos Division-Special Collections
        Rare Books Division-Special Collections
        Local History and Genealogy
        Staff: very large

        Prints and Photos Division has broadsides from 1804,
        1827, and 1864; caricatures from 1660, 1764, 1844;
        and lithographs from the 1830's. Rare Books has two
        volume photograph album of Prisoners in Mount Joy
        Prison in Dublin (1866), including American-born
        Irish imprisoned for political crimes. Local
        History and Genealogy has a three volume set of
        photographic views of NY City from the 1870's-1970's.
        Broadsides. Photos: criminals and crime, customs and
        celebrations, churches, neighborhoods, occupations,
        people, structures.

        Dates: 1660-1970's. Library.

        Hours: M-Sat 10-6 except Prints & Photos--M-Sat 1-6.
        Must obtain pass from Office of Special Collections.
        Open to the public. No admission or research fees.

        Loans for special exhibits. Fees for copy prints:
        $5 if negative exists, $17 if no negative.

                            +++++

NY63   STATEN ISLAND HISTORICAL SOCIETY

        441 Clarke Avenue
        Staten Island, NY 10306
        (718) 351-1617

        Charles L. Sachs, Chief Curator
        Staff: 35-40 full-time, 30 part-time; 100+ volunteer

        Kruser-Finlay House, though originally occupied by
        Irish-Americans, is not interpreted as
        Irish-American. St. Patrick's Church next to
        Richmond Restoration does have Irish connections.
        Structures, mill tools, oral history. Photos. Prior
        research suggested.

        100% catalogued. (Not by ethnic group.) Library.

        Hours: Office: M-F 9-5, Museum: W-F 10-5, Sat-Sun
        1-5. Appointment necessary. Open to serious
        researchers. $2.00 fee to use library.

        Loans for exhibits.
                            +++++

NY64   RENSSELAER COUNTY HISTORICAL SOCIETY

        59 2nd Street
        Troy, NY 12180
        (518) 272-7232

        Stacy Pomeroy Draper, Curator/Registrar
        Staff: 3 permanent, 50 volunteer

        Collection includes clothing, textile tools,
        woodworking tools, advertising media,
        religious objects, fraternal and social items.
        Photos: clubs and organizations, education, industry
        and commerce, military, structures, transportation.

        Not catalogued by ethnic group. Library.

        Hours: Office: M-F 9-5, Museum: T-Sat 10-4.
        Appointment not necessary but preferred. Open to
        qualified students and researchers. No admission or
        research fees.

        Loans for exhibits, upon review.

                             +++++

NC65   SOUTHERN APPALACHIAN HISTORICAL ASSSOCIATION

        P.O. Box 295
        Boone, NC 28607
        (704) 264-2120

        Curtis Smalling, Museum Director
        Staff: 8 permanent, 5 volunteer

        Collection includes structures, textile tools,
        woodworking tools.

        50% catalogued. Library.

        Hours: Summer Sun-W 6-8:30, Th-Sat 1-8:30; winter
        by appointment. Appointment necessary. Open to the
        public. No admission or research fees.

        Does not usually loan items.

                             +++++

OH66   WESTERN RESERVE HISTORICAL SOCIETY
        Library

        10825 East Boulevard
        Cleveland, OH 44106
        (216) 721-5722

        Dr. John Grabowski, Curator of Manuscripts
        Staff: 12, volunteer varies

OH66   (Western Reserve Historical Society)
cont.
         Manuscript collections include the Manning Collection
         of diaries and the Sullivan collection, which
         includes material on the Fenian movement. Library
         also has church histories. Photos: occupations.

         Catalogued.

         Hours: T-Sat 9-5. No appointment necessary. Open to
         the public. Fee for non-members.

         Loans from museum only under special conditions. No
         loans from library.

                         +++++

OR67   OREGON HISTORICAL SOCIETY

         1230 S.W. Park Avenue
         Portland, OR 97205
         (503) 222-1741

         Sue Seyl, Photo Librarian
         J. D. Cleaver, Curator of Collections
         Staff: 60 permanent, several hundred volunteers

         Collection includes photos, objects, structure,
         oral history. Prior research suggested.

         Catalogued. Library.

         Hours: Library: M-Sat 9:45-4:45, Museum: M-F
         9:45-4:45. Appointment not necessary. Open to the
         public. No research or admission fees.

         Loans under specific conditions.

                         +++++

PA68   THE BALCH INSTITUTE FOR ETHNIC STUDIES

         18 South Seventh Street
         Philadelphia, PA 19106
         (215) 925-8090

         Gail Stern, Museum Director
         David Sutton, Archivist
         Staff: 22 permanent, 15 volunteer

         The Balch has a traveling exhibit available--"Irish
         Eyes Still Smiling: Two Centuries in Philadelphia."
         Exhibit presents a social, economic, and political
         history of Philadelphia's past and present Irish
         community and includes 100 photographs.
         Collection includes contemporary Irish-American
         material as well as Irish song slides, a large

                                        Ohio-Pennsylvania

PA68   (The Balch Institute for Ethnic Studies)
cont.
         number of broadsides and caricatures, and sheet
         music. Also includes bedding, clothing, personal
         adornments, toys, fraternal and social organization
         items, peat from Ireland, map. Photos: customs and
         celebrations, entertainment, government, industry and
         commerce, music and dancing, neighborhoods,
         occupations, people, politics, structures,
         transportation, religion. Oral history.

         Catalogued. Library.

         Hours: Museum: M-Sat 10-4, Library: M-Sat 9-5.
         Appointment necessary. Open to the public.
         No admission or research fees.

         Loans for exhibits. Schedule of copy fees available.

                         +++++

PA69   THE HISTORICAL SOCIETY OF PENNSYLVANIA

         1300 Locust Street
         Philadelphia, PA   19107
         (215) 732- 6200

         Peter Parker, Director
         Linda Stanley, Manuscripts and Archives Curator
         Staff: 35 permanent

         Collection includes paintings by Irish-American
         artists and an engraved copper plate of a plan for
         the city of Philadelphia by Thomas Holme, an Irish
         immigrant and acting governor of Pennsylvania
         in the 1600's. Art objects, furniture, tools, maps.
         Photos: people.

         10% catalogued, 50% photographed. Library.

         Hours: Museum: T-F 9-5, Library: M 1-9, T-F 9-5.
         Appointment necessary for collections research. Open
         to the public. Manuscripts to serious researchers
         only. Fee for library.

         Loans for exhibits. Fee for copy prints: $20 for
         non-profit, $30 profit. Reproduction fees.

                         ++++++

PA70   INTERNATIONAL HOUSE
         Folklife Center

         3701 Chestnut Street
         Philadelphia, PA   19104
         (212) 387-5125 ext. 217

PA70   (International House)
cont.
         John Reynolds, Director
         Thomas McCabe, Technical Director
         Staff: 3 permanent

         Collection includes audio tapes which cover Irish
         culture and history, especially in Philadelphia and
         the Delaware Valley region. Tapes also document
         Irish musicians in performance. Photos:
         entertainment, music.

         Dates: Tapes--1977 to present. Collection is
         indexed.

         Hours: M-F 10-6. Appointment necessary. Open to
         the public. No admission or research fees.

         Loans for special exhibits.

                            +++++

PA71   LIBRARY COMPANY OF PHILADELPHIA
         Print Department

         1314 Locust
         Philadelphia, PA   19107
         (215) 546-2465

         Ken Finkel, Curator of Prints
         Staff: 14 permanent, 2 volunteer

         Collection includes broadsides, art objects,
         historical photos and advertisements. Check with
         other departments as well.

         Catalogued. Library.

         Hours: M-F 9-4:45. No appointment necessary. Open
         to the public. No research or admission fees.

         Loans for exhibits.

                            +++++

PA72   PHILADELPHIA MUSEUM OF ART

         Benjamin Franklin Parkway
         Box 7646
         Philadelphia, PA   19101-7646
         (215) 787-5408

         Jack Lindsey, American Art
         Staff: very large.

         Museum has extensive holdings of Irish and
         Irish-American paintings, furniture, and silver.

                                              Pennsylvania

PA72   (Philadelphia Museum of Art)
cont.
        Silver by Philip Syng, Irish craftsman.
        Collection includes furniture, food processing and
        service articles, art objects, period rooms.

        100% catalogued. Library.

        Hours: T-Sat 9-5. (Tu by appointment only.)
        Researchers must obtain written permission. Open to
        the public. Entrance fee.

        Loans for exhibits.

                         +++++

PA73   IRISH CENTRE OF PITTSBURGH

        6886 Forward Ave.
        Pittsburgh, PA 15217
        (412) 521-9712

        Eileen Minnock, Vice President
        Staff: 2 permanent, 1 volunteer

        Collection includes musical instruments, pottery,
        advertising media, religious objects, art objects,
        toys and dolls, fraternal and social organization
        items. Photos: advertisements, art, customs and
        celebrations. Oral history in process.

        Partially catalogued. Library.

        Hours by appointment. Appointment necessary. Open
        to students and researchers. No admission or
        research fees.

        No loans.

                         +++++

PA74   ECKLEY MINERS' VILLAGE

        Box 236, RR#2
        Weatherly, PA 18255
        (717) 636-2070

        Dr. David L. Salay, Director
        Staff: 8 permanent, 15 volunteer

        A living history museum of the daily and seasonal
        life of the anthracite miner and his family.
        Includes Church of the Immaculate Conception (1862),
        built primarily to serve the Irish. One of four
        museums and sites which preserve and interpret mining
        history. Collection includes structures, personal
        adornments, religious objects, broadsides, fraternal

PA74   (Eckley Miners' Village)
cont.
        and social organization items. Photographs:
        criminals and crime. An exhibit on immigrants is
        planned for 1987.

        Dates of photos: 1850-1986.

        Library. Not catalogued by Irish. Partially
        photographed.

        Hours: M-Sat 9-5, Sun 12-5. Appointment necessary.
        Library open to researchers. $2 fee to view
        collections.

        Loans if pre-insured and pre-arranged.

                            +++++

RI75   PROVIDENCE PUBLIC LIBRARY

        150 Empire Street
        Providence, RI   02903
        (401) 521-7722

        Lance J. Bauer, Special Collections Librarian
        Staff: 1 permanent, 1 volunteer

        Library has special collection--The George W. Potter
        and Alfred M. Williams Collection on Irish Culture.
        Includes nearly a thousand "slip ballads"
        (broadsides) from Ireland. Also has copy of the Book
        of Kells, and 450 pamphlets from 1740 to 1890.

        Dates: late 19th century.

        Indexed. Library.

        Hours: M, T, Th, F 9:30-1, 2-5. No appointment
        necessary. Serious researchers. No research or
        admission fees.

        Sometimes loans.

                            +++++

SC76   HIBERNIAN SOCIETY OF CHARLESTON SOUTH CAROLINA

        105 Meeting Street
        Charleston, SC   29401
        (803) 723-4752

        Carl S. Pulkinen, Historian
        Staff: 7 permanent

        The Hibernian Society was founded in 1799. Its

SC76   (Hibernian Society of Charleston South Carolina)
cont.
        members continue to meet, and hold an annual St.
        Patrick's Day celebration, making it one of the
        oldest sites of Irish-American fraternal
        organizations in the United States. Collection
        includes structures, art objects, minute books,
        photographs.

        Dates: 1799-present.

        Not catalogued. Library.

        Hours: Daily 11 AM -11 PM. Appointment necessary.
        Collection available to qualified researchers. No
        research or admission fees.

        No loans.

        Cf. HIBERNIAN HALL, SC130

                        +++++

TN77   TENNESSEE STATE MUSEUM

        505 Deaderick St.
        Nashville, TN 37219
        (615) 741-2692

        Stephen D. Cox, Curator of Cultural History
        Staff: 20 permanent, 50+ volunteer

        Collection includes food processing and service
        articles, art objects.

        1% catalogued. Photographed. Library.

        Hours: M-F 8-4:30; Museum: M-Sat 10-5, Sun 1-5. No
        appointment necessary. Library and collection open
        to staff, volunteers, and museum members. No
        research or admission fees.

        Loans for special exhibits.

                        +++++

TX78   INSTITUTE OF TEXAN CULTURES

        801 South Bowie
        P.O. Box 1226
        San Antonio, TX 78294
        (512) 226-7651

        Deborah Large, Director of Library Services
        Staff: Library--4 permanent, 12 volunteer

TX78   (Institute of Texan Cultures)
cont.
         Photos: agriculture, clothing, customs and
         celebrations, education, hotels, taverns, industry
         and commerce, military, music, neighborhoods,
         occupations, people, politics, immigrants,
         structures, transportation (railroad hand car),
         gravestones, towns settled by Irish, documents,
         signatures, cattle brand. Oral history. Exhibits.

         Dates: Photos: 1968-present.

         Photos catalogued by ethnic group. Library.

         Hours: Exhibits: T-Sun 9-5, Library: M-F 8-5.
         Appointment recommended. No research or admission
         fees.

         No loans. Fees for copy prints.

                                +++++

TX79   SAINT MARY'S CHURCH

         202 North Saint Mary's Street
         San Antonio, TX   78205
         (512) 226-8381

         Tom Harrell, Community Representative

         Saint Mary's Church is an old parish (1857),
         originally established for Germans in San Antonio,
         and later became an Irish parish. The church was
         rebuilt in 1924 and copied from Sacred Heart Church
         in Lowell, MA. Structure, photos, original records
         of Irish community in San Antonio. Photos include
         pictures of the Ancient Order of Hibernians.

         No library.

         Private church. Call for appointment. No research
         or admission fees. Open to the public.

         No loans.

         Cf. TEXAS IRISH FESTIVAL, TX163

                                +++++

VA80   VALENTINE MUSEUM

         1015 East Clay Street
         Richmond, VA   23219
         (804) 649-0711

         Gregg D. Kimball, Curator of Books and Manuscripts
         Staff: 20 permanent, 10 volunteer

VA80   (Valentine Museum)
cont.
         "There would be material relating to Irish Americans
         at the Valentine, but it would take extensive
         research to find it." Objects, photos. Prior
         research necessary.

         Library.

         Hours: M-F 10-5, Sat-Sun 1-5. Appointment
         necessary. Open to the public. No research or
         admission fees.

         Loans for exhibits.

                          +++++

WV81   WEST VIRGINIA STATE MUSEUM AND ARCHIVES

         Department of Culture and History
         The Cultural Center
         Capitol Complex
         Charleston, WV   25305
         (304) 348-0230

         Jan Luth, Museum
         Debra Basham, Archives
         Staff: 16 permanent, 10 volunteer

         Collections include objects, photographs and
         structures. Prior research necessary.

         Dates of photos: 1850's-1980's. Not catalogued by
         ethnic group.

         Library.

         Hours: M-Th 9-9, F 9-5, Sat 1-5. Appointment
         preferred. Open to the public. No research or
         admission fees.

         Loans under certain conditions for exhibits. Fees
         for copy prints. Some restrictions on use.

                          +++++

WI82   OLD WORLD WISCONSIN

         Route 2, Box 18
         Eagle, WI   53119
         (414) 594-2116

         Martin C. Perkins, Curator of Interpretation
         Staff: 8 permanent, 90 seasonal, 50-60 volunteer

WI82   (Old World Wisconsin)
cont.
        Collection includes the Mary Hafford House, built
        1885 in Hubbleton, WI for Mary Hafford, an Irish-born
        widow. Collection includes a wooden scrub top table,
        a wardrobe, and a small wooden trunk, all made by an
        Irish-American farmer. Also have bedding, furniture,
        lighting devices, clothing, personal adornments,
        toilet articles, food processing items, housekeeping
        tools, religious objects, structure.

        95% catalogued, 25% photographed. Library.

        Hours: Museum: May-June, Sept-Oct M-F 9-4,
        Sat-Sun 10-5; July-Aug 10-5 daily.
        Appointment necessary. Open to public. Fee for
        museum.

        Loans for exhibits.

                         +++++

WI83   STATE HISTORICAL SOCIETY OF WISCONSIN
        Visual and Sound Archives
        Museum

        816 State Street
        Madison, WI 53706
        (608) 262-3114

        Carol T. Larsen, Registrar
        Staff: Archives: 3 full-time, 15 part-time
                Museum: 21 permanent, volunteer varies

        Teacher supplement The Irish in Wisconsin is
        available. Tapes of interviews in the Irish
        community in Hubbleton, WI, are in Archives. (See
        WI81.) Collection includes broadsides, bedding,
        clothing, luggage, agricultural tools, food
        processing articles, tools, toys and dolls, fraternal
        and social organization items, containers, canes,
        letter opener. Photos: people, occupations (servant
        girls), structures, Ireland.

        Dates: early 19th century-present. Library.

        Hours: M-F 8-5. Appointment advised. Open to the
        public. No research or admission fees.

        Loans under special conditions for exhibits.

                         +++++

WI84   MILWAUKEE COUNTY HISTORICAL SOCIETY

        910 North 3rd Street
        Milwaukee, WI 53203
        (414) 273-8288
                                                    Wisconsin

WI84   (Milwaukee County Historical Society)
cont.
        Harry H. Anderson, Executive Director
        Staff: 9 permanent, 20 volunteer

        The Society is restoring the Jeremiah Curtin house
        in Greendale, WI which belonged to the well-known
        19th-century Irish-American linguist and diplomat,
        Jeremiah Curtin. Holdings include a ship's door
        from a famous shipwreck, the Lady Elgin, which
        involved nearly 300 residents of Milwaukee, most of
        them Irish-Americans. Structure, diaries, door from
        ship. Photos: people, structures.

        Library.

        Hours: M-F 9:30-12, 1-4:30. Appointment not
        necessary. Open to the public. Fees to view
        collection, use library.

        No loans.

        Cf. JEREMIAH CURTIN HOUSE, WI134

                            +++++

WI85   MILWAUKEE PUBLIC MUSEUM

        800 West Wells Street
        Milwaukee, WI   53233
        (414) 278-2751

        Dr. Lazar Brkich, Curator
        Staff: 167 permanent, 100 volunteer

        European village includes recreation of 19th-century
        Irish cottage with thatched roof. Structure,
        furniture, weapons, food processing and serving
        articles, housekeeping tools, musical instruments,
        textile tools, pottery, religious objects, art
        objects, toys and dolls, containers. Photos:
        clothing, customs and celebrations, entertainment,
        household interiors, music, people. Also contact
        Photographic Department.

        Objects catalogued. Library.

        Hours: Daily 9-4:45. Appointment necessary. Open
        to public. No fees for admission or research.

        Sometimes loans.

                            +++++

NF86   MEMORIAL UNIVERSITY OF NEWFOUNDLAND
        Folklore and Language Archive

        St. John's, Newfoundland,   A1C 5S7
        (709) 737-8402

        Philip Hiscock, Archivist
        Staff: 1 full-time, 6-10 part-time.

        This is a regional archive of folklore, folklife,
        oral history, and popular culture. Includes 10,000
        taped recordings, 12,000 photographs, and an artifact
        collection. "Since at least one-third of
        Newfoundlanders can trace their ancestry to Irish
        immigrants, MUNFLA is an archive of Irish North
        American Culture." Collection includes mummers'
        masks, tools, and models of traditional structures.
        Since collection is indexed by subject and not by
        ethnic group, prior research is suggested.

        Library.

        Hours: varies. Appointment necessary. Serious
        researchers. No admission or research fees.

        No loans. Limits on photocopying. Guide to use of
        the archive available.

                          +++++

NF87   THE PROVINCIAL ARCHIVES OF NEWFOUNDLAND AND LABRADOR

        Colonial Building
        Military Road
        St. John's, Newfoundland,   A1C 2C9

        (709) 753-9380

        Anthony P. Murphy, Archives Technician
        Staff: 12 permanent

        Collection includes the records of the Benevolent
        Irish Society of St. John's, founded 1806. Photos of
        many Irish communities in the Province, not broken
        down ethnically. Prior research necessary.

        Library.

        Hours: Winter 9-4:45 daily. Summer 9-4:15 daily. No
        appointment necessary. Open to any legitimate
        researcher. No research or admission fees.

        No loans.

                          +++++

                                        Newfoundland

ON88   NATIONAL MUSEUM OF MAN
        Canadian Centre for Folk Culture Studies

        Ottawa, Ontario,   KlA OM8
        (613) 997-8182

        George MacDonald, Director
        Dr. Paul Carpentier, Chief, Canadian Centre

        Large collection of fieldwork which includes
        materials from Irish-Canadians. Collections under
        the names: Boulton, Creighton, Cook, Doucette,
        Peacock, and Posen. Photographs, objects, oral
        history.

        Catalogued. Library.

        Hours: Museum: 10-5 daily, Office: M-F 8:15-4:30.

        Appointment necessary. Open to the public. No
        research or admission fees.

        Loans.

                            +++++

ON89   PUBLIC ARCHIVES CANADA
        National Photography Collection

        395 Wellington Street
        Ottawa, Ontario,   KlA ON3
        (613) 996-7801

        Louise Frechette, Public Service Section,
        Reference Consultant
        Staff: very large

        The National Photography Collection consists of some
        8.5 million photographs. The collection is indexed
        in The Guide to Canadian Photographic Archives,
        which may be ordered from the address listed below.
        Photos related to the Irish in Canada include:
        disasters, foodways, military, people, structures,
        travel, immigration and immigrants. Subjects include
        the quarantine station building in Grosse Ile,
        Quebec, used for immigrants fleeing the famine in
        Ireland; the memorial erected in 1909 in
        commemoration of the famine victims; an Irish
        settler's farm in Saskatchewan in 1927; Irish
        immigrants; and a ship's company from Northern
        Ireland in 1945.

        Catalogued. Library.

        Hours: M-F 8:30-4. Appointment suggested. Open to
        the public. No research or admission fees.

                                              Ontario

ON89   (Public Archives Canada)
cont.
       A guide to the collection and a schedule of copy fees
       is available on request. Write to: Canadian
       Government Publishing Centre, Supply and Services
       Canada, Ottawa, Canada K1A 0S9 for the main guide to
       the archives. $35 in Canada, $42 in other
       countries.

       Cf. CELTIC CROSS, QU134.

                        +++++

PE90   PRINCE EDWARD ISLAND MUSEUM AND HERITAGE FOUNDATION

       2 Kent Street
       Charlottetown, Prince Edward Island, C1A 1M6

       Trude Oliver, Curator of Collections
       Staff: 15 permanent, 4 volunteer

       Collection includes a badge from the Ancient Order of
       Hibernians, silver, a vest and stole from the
       Benevolent Irish Society, and several hand-made
       towels and domestic items. Also personal
       adornments, food processing and service articles,
       pottery, transportation, advertising media, fraternal
       and social organization items, sheet music, Bible.
       95% catalogued. Library.

       Hours: Winter 8:30-5; Summer 8-4. Appointment
       necessary. Open to staff and researchers. No
       research or admission fees.

       Loans for special exhibits.

                        +++++

CHAPTER II
National Register Sites

This chapter describes National Register sites of Irish American significance. The entries were abstracted from the 1976 edition of the National Register of Historic Places, which is complete through the end of 1974. Additional entries were suggested by materials listed in the bibliography. Three National Historic Sites from Canada with Irish significance are listed as well.

Cross-references to other entries are indicated where a direct overlap or correspondence of holdings exists, or where the entries are very closely related.

AL91   VALLEY CREEK PRESBYTERIAN CHURCH

        Valley Creek Road
        Selma, AL   36701

        1857-1858

        Built to serve one of the state's oldest
        Presbyterian congregations, which was organized
        by eight Scotch-Irish families from North Carolina.

        Private.

                            +++++

CA 92   JAMES C. FLOOD MANSION

        California and Mason Streets
        San Francisco, CA   94108

        1886

        One of two houses designed by Augustus Laver for
        James C. Flood, Irish immigrant and "bonanza king"
        of the Comstock Lode in Nevada. The only Nob Hill
        mansion to survive the 1906 earthquake and fire.
        This area was home to several wealthy Irish-
        Americans in the 1800's. House is now occupied
        by the Pacific Union Club.

        Private: not accessible to the public.

        Historic American Building Survey

                            +++++

CO93   MOLLY BROWN HOUSE

        1340 Pennsylvania Street
        Denver, CO   80203

        1887-1892

        Home to mining millionaire "Johnny" Brown and his
        wife Molly. Molly was an Irish immigrant and a
        colorful international socialite nicknamed
        "Unsinkable" after surviving the 1912 sinking of
        the Titanic. Not interpreted as Irish.

        Private. Museum.

                            +++++

DE94   FISHER'S PARADISE (PARADISE POINT)

        624 Pilottown Road
        Lewes, DE   19958
                                  Alabama-Delaware (Sites)

DE94   (Fisher's Paradise)
cont.
          Early 18th-century colonial house owned by Dr. Henry
          Fisher, an Irish immigrant and the area's first
          physician of note.

          Private; not accessible to public.

                              +++++

DE95   BRANDYWINE MANUFACTURERS' SUNDAY SCHOOL

          Wilmington, DE 19807

          1817

          Built with donations from Eleuthere Irenee DuPont as
          school for working children and adults, many of them
          Irish immigrants and descendants. Part of the Hagley
          Museum complex.

          Private; museum.

          Cf. HAGLEY MUSEUM, DE 6.
              ELEUTHERIAN MILLS, DE 96.
              ST. JOSEPH'S ON THE BRANDYWINE, DE97.

                              +++++

DE96   ELEUTHERIAN MILLS

          Wilmington, DE 19807

          19th-century mill complex includes the DuPont
          original residence, an office building, an 1858
          machine mill, and the remains of 21 powder mills.
          Established by E. I. DuPont, a French immigrant, the
          factory was the largest explosives factory in the
          country by 1810. Many of the powder workers were
          Irish immigrants whose passage had been paid by
          the DuPont Company.

          Private. Museum.

          National Historic Landmark

          Cf. HAGLEY MUSEUM, DE 6.

                              +++++

DE97   ST. JOSEPH'S ON THE BRANDYWINE

          10 Barley Mill Road
          Wilmington, DE 19807

          1841

DE97   (St. Joseph's on the Brandywine)
cont.
         Built by the DuPont family for their Irish and
         Italian Catholic workers. When the church was
         consecrated in 1894, it was the largest Catholic
         church in the state. Many Irish immigrants are
         buried in the church cemetary.

         Private

         Cf. HAGLEY MUSEUM, DE 6.

                        +++++

DC98   GEORGETOWN UNIVERSITY ASTRONOMICAL OBSERVATORY

         37th and O Streets, NW
         Georgetown University
         Washington DC   20057

         1841-1844

         Designed by Father James Curley, this is the third
         oldest American observatory. Directed in the 1880's
         by Fr. John Hagen, a prominent astronomer.
         Georgetown University was founded in 1789 by Bishop
         John Carroll and represents early Irish-Catholic
         higher education.

         Private.

                        +++++

IL99   ST. PATRICK'S ROMAN CATHOLIC CHURCH

         718 West Adams Street
         Chicago, IL   60606

         1856

         The oldest church building in Chicago, and one of
         the few which survived the Great Chicago Fire in
         1871. Includes stained glass designed by Thomas
         O'Shaughnessy in 1911. Many of the interior
         decorations are based on designs from the Book of
         Kells. Parish was established in 1846 and served a
         mostly Irish congregation. Still an important
         center of Irish activities in Chicago.

         Private.

         Cf. ARCHDIOCESE OF CHICAGO ARCHIVES, IL13.

                        +++++

                              Delaware-Illinois (Sites)

KY100   ST. JOSEPH ROMAN CATHOLIC CHURCH

         430 Church Street
         Bowling Green, KY   42101

         1870-1884

         Congregation was organized in 1859 to serve the many
         Irish Catholics engaged in building the Louisville
         and Nashville Railroads. Frank Kister Sr. and Jr.,
         architects.

         Private.

                              +++++

KY101   FELIX GRIMES HOUSE

         1301 Leitchfield Road
         Owensboro, KY   42303

         1867-1876

         Home of Felix Grimes, Irish immigrant, geologist,
         and proprietor of several local coal mines.

         Private; not accessible to the public.

                              +++++

LA102   ST. ALPHONSUS CHURCH

         2029 Constance Street
         New Orleans, LA   70130

         1855

         One of three churches built by the priests of the
         congregation of The Most Holy Redeemer. Built for
         the city's Irish Catholic congregation. Louis Long,
         architect. Brick.

         Private.
                              +++++

ME103   ST. JOHN'S CATHOLIC CHURCH

         York Street
         Bangor, ME   04401

         1855

         Built to serve Bangor's Irish community despite
         Nativist opposition from Know Nothings. Patrick C.
         Keeley, architect. Brick--Gothic revival.

         Private.
                              +++++
                                   Kentucky-Maine (Sites)

ME104   ST. DENIS CATHOLIC CHURCH

         ME 218
         North Whitefield, ME   04353

         1833

         Second oldest Catholic Church in the state and one
         of the oldest in New England. This area was settled
         in the early 19th century by Irish immigrants.

         Private.

                             +++++

MD105   CARROLL MANSION

         800 East Lombard Street
         Baltimore, MD   21202

         1811-1812

         Final home of Charles Carroll, a signer of the
         Declaration of Independence, and grandson of Charles
         Carroll an Irish immigrant and the attorney general
         for the third Lord Baltimore, Charles Calvert.
         Carroll was an early member of Congress and one of
         the founders of the Baltimore and Ohio Railroad.

         Museum, Municipal.

         Historic American Buildings Survey.

         Cf. BALTIMORE CITY LIFE MUSEUMS, MD26.

                             +++++

MD106   OLD ROMAN CATHOLIC CATHEDRAL (MINOR BASILICA)

         401 Cathedral Street
         Baltimore, MD   21201

         1806-1863

         Designed by Benjamin Henry Latrobe, this is the
         first Roman Catholic Cathedral built in the United
         States. It is built in a Latin-cross shape and
         considered an "extraordinary" structure. Archbisop
         John Carroll, member of an early Maryland
         Irish-Catholic family, laid the cornerstone and is
         buried here. Designated a minor basilica in 1936.

         Private.

         Historic American Buildings Survey.
         National Historic Landmark.

                             +++++
                                    Maine-Maryland (Sites)

MD107   ST.FRANCIS XAVIER CHURCH (OLD BOHEMIA)

        MD 299
        NW Warwick, MD   21912

        1792

        Early site of Jesuit mission in MD, associated withx
        Archbishop John Carroll.

        Private; Museum.

        Historic American Buildings Survey.

                            +++++

 MA108 ST. STEPHEN'S CHURCH

        401 Hanover Street
        Boston, MA   02113

        1804

        Designed by Charles Bullfinch. Originally the New
        North Church, this was a Congregational parish, then
        Unitarian, and finally Catholic. Became the parish
        for many of Boston's wealthy Irish in the 1860's,
        including the Fitzgeralds, John F. Kennedy's
        maternal side. Church reflects the changing ethnic
        and religious character of the North End of Boston.
        Restored in 1965 by Cardinal Cushing.

        Private.

                            +++++

MI109   FEODAR PROTAR CABIN

        SW of St. James
        Beaver Island, MI   49782

        1860

        A hewn log cabin built by an Irish settler. Later
        the home of Feodar Protar, who provided free medical
        supplies to the islanders.

        Private; not accessible to the public.

                            +++++

MN110   CHURCH OF ST. BRIDGET

        Third Street and Ireland Avenue
        De Graff, MN   56233

        1901

MN110   (Church of St. Bridget)
cont.
         St. Bridget was the first parish established as part
         of St. Paul Archbishop John Ireland's efforts at
         colonizing western Minnesota with Irish immigrants.
         The first church in the parish was built in 1876 and
         later replaced by the current building. Area is
         still heavily Irish Catholic and St. Bridget's is
         the only church in De Graff. Designed by St. Paul
         architect Edward J. Donahue. Gothic Revival build-
         ing made of red brick.

         Private.

                          +++++

NV111   AUSTIN HISTORIC DISTRICT

         In Pony Canyon,
         Junction of U.S. 50 and NV 8A
         Austin, NV 89310

         19th century

         Mining town containing 1 and 2 story commercial,
         residential, government, and religious structures of
         brick, stone, and frame. The town grew quickly
         after the discovery of silver ore in 1862. The
         population reached 2,000 in 1863 and included many
         English and Irish immigrants.

         Multiple public/private.

                          +++++

NJ112   EUGENE V. KELLY CARRIAGE HOUSE

         South Orange Avenue
         Seton Hall University Campus
         South Orange, NJ   07079

         1887

         Built for Eugene V. Kelly, an Irish immigrant and
         successful merchant, investor, and patron of Seton
         Hall University. John E. Baker, architect.

         Private.
                          +++++

NY113   ST. JAMES CHURCH

         32 James Street
         New York, NY 10038

         1837

NY113   (St. James Church)
cont.

Established by an Irish congregation, its pastor
Father John Smith and his assistant, Father Mark
Murphy, both died of cholera assisting famine
immigrants in the 1840's. A branch of St. Patrick's
Funeral Benefit Society was established there in
1836 and later became the Ancient Order of
Hibernians. Plaque which commemorates the
centennial of the AOH in America was put in the
church in 1936. Oldest Catholic structure in New
York.

Private.

                              +++++

NY114   ST. PATRICK'S CATHEDRAL

Fifth Avenue at 50th
New York, NY   10011

1858-1879

Designed by James Renwick. Construction was
interrupted by the Civil War. Dedicated by John
Cardinal McCloskey. Associated with New York's
Irish community from its beginning to the present.
Annual site of New York's St. Patrick's Day Parade.

Private.

                              +++++

NY115   UNION STREET HISTORIC DISTRICT

Union Street
Poughkeepsie, NY   12601

19th century

Working-class, urban neighborhood containing 173
historical commercial and residential structures.
Poughkeepsie's oldest section, which was settled
largely by Irish, German, Italian, and Slavic
immigrants and Blacks.

Multiple public/private.

                              +++++

OH116   HOLY NAME HIGH SCHOOL

8318 Broadway
Cleveland, OH   44105

1873

OH116   (Holy Name High School)
cont.
         First Catholic building in the former town of
         Newburgh, the steel center of Cleveland. Had large
         Slavic and Irish Catholic populations.

         Private.

                         +++++

OH117   DEAN FAMILY FARM

         Ballard Road
         Jamestown OH   45335

         1815-1833

         First farmed by Irish immigrant and pioneer settler,
         Daniel Dean, ca. 1812. Occupied by eight
         generations of the Dean family.

         Private; not accessible to the public.

                         +++++

OK118   JAMES H. McBIRNEY HOUSE

         1414 South Galveston
         Tulsa, OK   74127

         1927

         Built for Irish immigrant James H. McBirney,
         wealthy banker and developer. John Long, builder.

         Private.

                         +++++

PA119   JAMES MILLER HOUSE

         Manse Drive
         Bethel, PA   19507

         1808, 1830

         Built in two sections by James Miller and his son on
         site of original log structure built by Irish
         immigrant Oliver Miller, c. 1763. Site of the
         first shot fired in the 1792 Whiskey Rebellion.
         Good example of early Western Pennsylvania domestic
         architecture. Stone and rubble masonry
         construction.

         County.

                         +++++

PA120   DANIEL BOONE HOMESTEAD SITE AND BERTOLET CABIN

Birdsboro, PA 19508

18th century

Birthplace of Daniel Boone, descendent of 18th-
century Irish immigrants, and well-known explorer
and pioneer. Fieldstone house built on the site of
the Boone family log cabin. Boone was born in 1734
and was a member of an Ulster Scots family.

Private. Museum.

+++++

PA121   NICHOLAS NEWLIN HOUSE

Concord Road
Concordville, PA   19331

1742

Built by Nicholas Newlin, an Irish immigrant who
became active in regional political and business
affairs. Brick.

Private.

+++++

PA122   DOBBIN HOUSE

89 Steinwehr Avenue
Gettysburg, PA   17325

1776

One of Gettysburg's oldest structures; built by
Reverend Alexander Dobbin, an Irish missionary. It
served as his home, a classical academy, a
theological seminary, and sometimes a church.
Made of random stone set in mortar.

Private.

+++++

PA123   GETTYSBURG BATTLEFIELD HISTORIC DISTRICT

Gettysburg, PA   17325

1863

The Irish Brigade took part in the July Battle of
Gettysburg, and their valor is commemorated with a
monument which displays a Celtic Cross and a
mourning wolfhound.

Pennsylvania (Sites)

PA123   (Gettysburg Battlefield Historic District)
cont.
          Multiple public/private.

                         +++++

PA124   GREAT CONEWAGO PRESBYTERIAN CHURCH

          Church Road
          Hunterstown, PA   17325

          1787

          One of the area's earliest churches organized by
          Scotch-Irish settlers. Built of fieldstone.
          Georgian style.

          Private.

                         +++++

PA125   GUINSTON UNITED PRESBYTERIAN CHURCH

          Laurel, PA   17400

          1733

          The simple conservative form and detailing of this
          church symbolizes the religious beliefs and
          lifestyles of the Scotch-Irish settlers it
          served. Stone and brick.

          Private.

                         +++++

PA126   ST. AUGUSTINE'S CATHOLIC CHURCH

          4th and New Streets
          Philadelphia, PA   19106

          1847

          Built on ruins of original church burned by
          anti-Catholic, anti-Irish demonstraters in 1844.
          Napoleon LeBrun and Edward F. Durang, architects.

          Private.

                         +++++

PA127   OBELISK OF HONOR

          Valley Forge, PA   19481

          1985

PA127   (Obelisk of Honor)
cont.
         Dedicated to foreign-born recipients of the
         Congressional Medal of Honor, including sixty-five
         Irish-born. Obelisk is made of Wicklow granite
         from Ireland and was donated by the Ancient Order
         of Hibernians in America in 1985. Honors foreign-
         born soldiers from the Civil and Indian Wars.

                              +++++

RI128   FORMER IMMACULATE CONCEPTION CHURCH

         119 High Street
         Westerly, RI   02891

         1886-1889

         City's first Roman Catholic church, serving Irish
         and Italian immigrants. Gothic revival. Frame with
         clapboarding.

         Private.

                              +++++

RI129   CATO HILL HISTORIC DISTRICT

         RI 44
         Woonsocket, RI   02895

         1838-1900

         A primarily mid-19th-century working-class
         neighborhood occupied successively by Irish,
         French-Canadian, and Ukrainian immigrants. The
         settlement reflects the industrial expansion of the
         city of Woonsocket.

         Multiple use/private.

                              +++++

SC130   HIBERNIAN HALL

         105 Meeting Street
         Charleston, SC   29401

         1840

         The Hibernian Society was organized in 1799 by eight
         Irishmen who met as a social club and to raise
         money for emigrants from Ireland. The hall was
         opened in 1841 and became historically significant
         during the 1860 Democratic Convention when Stephen
         Douglas's delegation was housed there. The

SC130   (Hibernian Hall)
cont.
         Democrats split on choosing a candidate and ensured
         a victory for Abraham Lincoln and the Republican
         party. Today the society has a membership of 325
         and the presidency alternates between a Catholic and
         Protestant member. A St. Patrick's Day celebration
         is held every year in the Hall.

         Private.

         National Historic Landmark.

         Cf. HIBERNIAN SOCIETY OF CHARLESTON, SC76.

                         +++++

TN131   GREENEVILLE HISTORIC DISTRICT

         Greeneville, TN 37743

         18th-20th century

         Business district flanked by residential area.
         Contains numerous commercial, residential, and
         religious structures. Area was settled by
         Scotch-Irish after 1783 and is named after
         Revolutionary War general Nathanael Greene.

         Multiple public/private.

         Historic American Buildings Survey.

                         +++++

TX132   JAMES MCGLOIN HOMESTEAD

         FM 666
         NW of San Patricio, TX   78350

         1855

         Built by James McGloin who was involved in the
         colonization of Irish families in the area. Frame,
         clapboarding.

         Private; not accessible to the public.

                         +++++

WV133   SLOAN-PARKER HOUSE

         US 50
         East of Junction, W VA   26824

         1790

WV133   (Sloan-Parker House)
cont.
         Built for Scotch-Irish immigrant Richard Sloan, who
         carried on a weaving business here. Served as early
         19th-century stage stop along the Northern
         Turnpike, from 1860 to 1910. House is made of
         fieldstone and includes a log smokehouse and barn,
         c. 1803.

         Private.

                           +++++

WI134   JEREMIAH CURTIN HOUSE

         8685 West Grange Avenue
         Greendale, WI   53129

         1846-1847

         Birthplace of Jeremiah Curtin, author, linguist,
         and son of Irish immigrants. Curtin collected
         material on immigrant and Indian folklore and was
         member of the US Diplomatic Corps. House is being
         restored by the Milwaukee County Historical Society.

         Private.

         Historic American Buildings Survey.

         Cf. MILWAUKEE COUNTY HISTORICAL SOCIETY, WI84.

                           +++++

NB135   CELTIC CROSS

         Partridge Island
         Saint John, New Brunswick

         1927

         Cross erected in the memory of 15,000 Irish
         immigrants, who came here fleeing the Famine in
         Ireland in 1847. Thousands died of typhus at this
         quarantine station.

         National Historic Site.

                           +++++

ON136   RIDGEWAY BATTLEFIELD

         Ridgeway, Ontario

         1929

ON136   (Ridgeway Battlefield)
cont.

          Plaque to the memory of the officers and men who
          fought here against Fenian Raiders from the
          United States on June 2, 1866.

          National Historic Site.

                              +++++

QU137   CELTIC CROSS

          Grosse Ile, Quebec

          The Grosse Ile quarantine station was established
          in 1832 to prevent outbreaks of cholera from
          immigrants to Canada. In spite of the quarantine
          station, cholera and typhus spread throughout Canada
          on a number of occasions. Cross was built to the
          memory of the thousands of Irish immigrants who
          passed through here fleeing the Famine in Ireland.

          National Historic Site.

          Cf. PUBLIC ARCHIVES CANADA, ON89.

                              +++++

CHAPTER III

Festivals

This chapter describes festivals in the United States and Canada which include primarily Irish, or in some cases, Celtic, events. Information for these listings was obtained through written and oral surveys. Each listing includes the name of the festival, its location, a contact person, a description of events, a brief history of the festival, annual dates, audience size, and whether photographs of events are available to researchers.

As with collections of materials, the researcher should always call in advance to make sure that dates and location of festivals have not changed. These listings represent only a sampling of the many celebrations of Irish culture in North America, ranging from small and local ceilis to huge international festivals and feisanna.

AZ138   PHOENIX IRISH FEIS

St. Gregory Parish Grounds

Lorraine Flynn
1710 West Camelback Road
Phoenix, AZ   85020
(602) 939-1183

Sponsor: Valley Irish Clubs

The Phoenix Feis began in 1984 with support of the
valley Irish organizations. Its sole purpose is to
promote and encourage all forms of Irish culture.
A Civil War "Irish Brigade" sets up camp on
the grounds each year. Ceili held on Saturday night
and Gaelic Mass on Sunday. Includes step dancing
competition, folk dancing, music, crafts, food,
gaelic football, and Irish cultural heritage room.

Dates: Last weekend in October.
Open to the public. Audience size: 4,000.
Photographs available to researchers.

+++++

CA139   GRAND NATIONAL IRISH FAIR AND MUSIC FESTIVAL

The Rose Bowl

Catherine F. Kay
Irish Fair Foundation
P.O. Box 341
Pasadena, CA   91102

Sponsor: Irish Fair Foundation of Southern
California, Inc.

Begun in 1974 at Notre Dame High School as a small
ethnic fair. Grown to large festival held in the
Rose Bowl. Includes Irish step dance, Scottish
dance, ceili dance, harp and fiddle competition,
Irish foods; and crafts, including spinning,
weaving, wool carding. Costumes displayed in Tara
Village from 2nd century BC to 16th century AD.
Gaelic Mass on Sunday.

Dates: Second weekend in June.
Open to the public. Audience size: 30,000.
Photographs available to researchers.

+++++

CO140   LONG'S PEAK SCOTTISH HIGHLANDS FESTIVAL

Rocky Mountain National Park

CO140   (Long's Peak Scottish Highlands Festival)
cont.
         Dr. Jim Derwood
         P.O. Box 1820
         Estes Park, CO   80517
         (800) 621-5888

         This festival was begun in 1976 to educate people
         about Celtic cultures. It includes champion step
         dancers from Ireland, a pub crawl, a cattle show,
         and the Glenlivet Drum Major competition for
         drumming corps. Festival begins Friday night with
         folk band competition and goes through Sunday.
         Sunday includes an interdenominational prayer
         breakfast. Also guest bands from Scotland and
         Canada, craft displays, food and children's area.

         Dates: First weekend after Labor Day.
         Open to the public. Audience size: 10-20,000.
         Photographs available to researchers.

                          +++++

CT141   GREATER HARTFORD IRISH FESTIVAL

         Grounds of Irish American Home

         Mike Connolly
         The Irish American Home
         132 Glastonbury Street
         Glastonbury, CT   06033
         (203) 666-0022

         Sponsor: The Irish American Home Society Inc.

         Festival was started in 1984 and is held on the
         Irish American Home Club grounds. This is a family
         gathering. Includes Irish stepdancing by three
         local dance schools, Irish and American music,
         basketweaving and crochet, corned beef dinners, a
         Miss Irish Festival, Mass on Sunday with local
         singers, a cultural tent, and children's games.

         Dates: Last weekend in July.
         Open to the public. Audience: 5-8,000.
         No photographs available.

                          +++++

DE142   ANNUAL FEIS

         Concord High School Grounds

                                   Colorado-Delaware (Festivals)

DE142   (Annual Feis)
cont.
         Bob McHugh
         Irish Culture Club of Delware
         P.O. Box 9326
         Wilmington, DE   19809
         (302) 478-2819

         Sponsor: Irish Culture Club of Delaware

         This feis was started as an annual cultural event
         by members of the Irish Culture Club in 1977.
         It includes step-dancing and music competitions
         by dancers and musicians from around the United
         States and Canada. It also includes craft
         competitions and Irish food. Two Masses are held
         the day of the feis. Although it was not held in
         1987, plans are to continue the feis in 1988.

         Dates: 3rd Sunday in August.
         Open to the public. Audience: 2,000.
         Slides available to researchers.

                          +++++

 IL143   IRISH FEST

         Olive Park

         Mike Shevlin
         Irish American Heritage Center
         4626 Knox Avenue
         Chicago, IL   60630
         (312) 282-7035

         Formerly called Irish Family Days, the fest is
         co-sponsored by the Irish American Heritage Center
         and Gaelic Park. Includes local and international
         performers, step dancers from local schools, and a
         cultural heritage tent. Also crafts booths, Irish
         food, a Children's Stage, and a grand prize of a
         trip to Ireland. Mass on Sunday.

         Dates: First weekend in August.
         Open to the public. Audience: 68,000 in 1986.
         Photographs available to researchers.

                          +++++

 KY144   IRISH HERITAGE WEEKEND

         Riverfront Plaza

         Penny Stetman
         Heritage Corporation
         1 Riverfront Plaza
         Lousville, KY   40202
         (502) 566-5068

KY144   (Irish Heritage Weekend)
cont.
         Sponsor: Heritage Corporation

         The Heritage Corporation was originally a
         Bicentennial committee which was formed to promote
         the ethnic heritage of Louisville. It began having
         ethnic weekends in 1979. The Irish weekend includes
         local and national dance and music groups, crafts,
         food and cultural displays. Also sponsors a St.
         Patrick's Day Parade.

         Dates: Weekend in the summer. Varies.
         Open to the public. Audience: 80-100,000.
         Photographs available to researchers.

                            +++++

MD145   BALTIMORE IRISH FESTIVAL

         Festival Hall

         Carmel Gambacorta
         Baltimore Office of Tourism
         34 Market Place
         Baltimore, MD 21222
         (301) 837-4636

         Sponsors: 10 Irish clubs in Baltimore

         Begun in 1972, this festival was started by Larry
         Smith to promote Irish culture. Includes a ceili
         on Friday night and a Catholic Mass on Sunday.
         Local singers, bands and dancers. Clubs sell Irish
         food, and vendors have to sell Irish materials. In
         1986, had achora (Irish rowboats) teams from
         Galway, New York, Boston, and Pittsburgh in the
         Harbor.

         Dates: September
         Open to the public. Audience: 15,000+.
         No photographs available.

                            +++++

MA146   FITCHBURG IRISH FESTIVAL

         Wallace Civic Center

         Bob O'Connell
         P.O. Box 236
         Fitchburg MA   01420
         617-342-7882

         Sponsor: Irish American Association of Fitchburg

MA146   (Fitchburg Irish Festival)
cont.
         This festival was begun seven years ago, and is
         claimed to be the first Irish Festival in New
         England. An Irish Soda bread contest is held
         annually. Includes demonstrations of Irish step
         dancing plus Irish country dancing by the audience.
         There is also an Irish pub, music from local bands,
         imported Irish goods and crafts, and Irish and
         American foods. A Mass begins the festival.
         Trip to Ireland offered in a raffle with an Irish
         weekend in Cape Cod as a door prize.

         Dates: Second Sunday of July.
         Open to the public.
         Photographs available to researchers.

                             +++++

MA147   NEW ENGLAND IRISH FESTIVAL

         Sullivan Stadium

         Brian O'Donovan
         Route 1
         Foxboro, MA   02035
         (617) 262-1776

         Sponsor: Stadium Management Corporation

         This festival began in 1984. The Stadium is owned
         by an Irish-American family who wanted to create a
         family event. Includes an Irish cottage, a
         children's area, Gaelic games, step dancing, and
         local and international musicians. Also has a
         cultural area sponsored by the Inter-Celtic
         Society and Irish food.

         Dates: 2nd or last weekend in June.
         Open to the public. Audience: 25,000.
         Photographs available to researchers.

                             +++++

MI148   IRISH FESTIVAL OF DETROIT

         Waterfront Plaza

         Chris Murray
         2068 Michigan Avenue
         Detroit, MI   48216
         (313) 963-8895

         Sponsor: Gaelic League and Irish American Club of
                  Detroit

                             Massachusetts-Michigan (Festivals)

MI148   (Irish Festival of Detroit)
cont.
         The festival was organized in 1971 by the Gaelic
         League to promote Irish culture. League holds
         weekly dance classes and music programs as well.
         Festival includes step dancing, music, crafts,
         food, and a Mass on Sunday at noon. Has an ethnic
         gallery with a different topic each year. Theme for
         1987 was "The Irish in Michigan--150 Years."

         Dates: 1st weekend in June.
         Open to the public. Audience: 20,000.
         Photographs available to researchers.

                          +++++

MN149   MINNESOTA IRISH FESTIVAL

         Ellen Rang
         Box 75584
         St. Paul MN   55175
         (612) 722-3954

         Sponsor: Minnesota Irish Festival Inc.

         Festival started in 1979 by Roger Conway and local
         Irish-Americans who wanted to promote Irish culture.
         Includes dance lessons, ceili, performances; music

         by local and national, and international
         performers. Also has crafts, food, historical and
         modern costumes, and a Gaelic Mass on Sunday.

         Dates: Second weekend in August.
         Open to the public. Audience: 20,000 in 1985.
         Photographs available to researchers.

                          +++++

NJ150   IRISH FESTIVAL

         Garden State Arts Center

         Jay Scott
         534 Washington Boulevard
         Seagirt, NJ 08750
         (201) 449-1338

         Sponsor: Irish Festival Foundation Inc.

         This festival began in 1970 to promote Irish music
         and dance. It includes a bagpipe competition in the
         morning followed by a Mass. The afternoon program
         includes step dancing, music, and cultural exhibits.
         Irish foods and Gaelic football are also offered.
         Most of the performers are from New Jersey, although
         some performers from Ireland also attend.

                              Michigan-New Jersey (Festivals)

NJ150   (Irish Festival)
cont.
         Dates: Last Sunday in June.
         Open to the public. Audience: 20,000
         Material available to researchers.

                        +++++

NY151   EMPIRE STATE IRISH FESTIVAL

         Empire State Plaza

         Randy Lynch
         91 Quail Street
         Albany, NY 12206
         (518) 489-3144

         Sponsor: Capital District Council AOH

         This festival began in 1977. Includes set dancing,
         step dancing, a bagpipe band, Irish American show
         bands, crafts, food, and drink.

         Dates: August.
         Open to the public. Audience 10-12,000.
         Photographs available to researchers.

                        +++++

NY152   THE GREAT IRISH FAIR

         Steeple Chase Park
         Coney Island

         Al O'Hagen
         2750 Gerritsen Avenue
         Brooklyn, NY 11229
         (718) 403-2580

         Sponsor: Ancient Order of Hibernians and Brooklyn
                  Borough President's Office

         Festival was started in 1981. Serves as a
         fundraiser for Brooklyn Catholic Charities.
         Includes step dancing, music, Gaelic sports, arts
         and crafts, children's games, and Irish food.

         Dates: First weekend after Labor Day.
         Open to the public. Audience size: 1 million.
         Photographs available to researchers.

                        +++++

NY153   BUFFALO IRISH FESTIVAL

         Weimer's Grove
         Lancaster, NY
                              New Jersey-New York (Festivals)

NY153   (Buffalo Irish Festival)
cont.
        Kevin Townsell
        4230 Genessee Street
        Cheektowaga, NY   14225
        (716) 632-8400

        Sponsor: Liffey Productions

        Festival began in 1982 as an offshoot of Irish music
        programs held at the Shannon Pub. Benefits seven
        Buffalo Irish organizations. Includes shows by four
        Irish step dancing schools, folk-oriented Irish
        bands from New England, Buffalo area, and Ontario,
        Canada. Regional crafts, Irish stew, corned beef
        and cabbage, children's tent.

        Dates: Weekend before Labor Day.
        Open to the public. Audience: 8-10,000.
        No photos available to researchers.

                          +++++

NY154   INTERNATIONAL CELTIC FESTIVAL

        Hunter Mountain

        Don Conover
        Bridge Street
        Hunter, NY   12442
        (518) 263-3800

        Sponsor: Exposition Planners

        Started in 1981. Includes step dancing, music,
        crafts, food, Highland games, and pipe bands
        representing Irish, Welsh, and Scottish cultures.
        Pipe bands have a mass march down the side of the
        mountain. Performers are both local and
        international.

        Dates: mid-August.

        Open to the public. Audience: 5-6,000.
        Photographs available to researchers.

                          +++++

NY155   IRISH MUSIC FESTIVAL

        Snug Harbor Cultural Center
        Staten Island

NY155   (Irish Music Festival)
cont.
         Rebecca Miller
         Irish Arts Center
         553 West 51st Street
         New York, NY 10019
         (212) 757-3318

         Sponsor: Irish Arts Center

         Festival has been held since 1982. Includes step
         dance performances, ceili dancing, traditional music

         performance and workshops, crafts, and Irish food.

         Dates: Last Saturday in June.
         Open to the public. Audience: 3,000.
         No photographs available to researchers.

                              +++++

NY156   UNITED IRISH COUNTIES ASSOCIATION FEIS

         St. Joseph's Seminary
         Yonkers NY

         United Irish Counties Association
         738 8th Avenue
         Suite 2C
         New York, NY 10036
         (212) 265-4226

         Sponsor: United Irish Counties Association of NY

         Begun in 1932, the feis is organized and carried on
         for the purpose of promoting Irish cultural activity
         in the United States. Offers competition for
         amateurs in a wide range of Irish traditions from
         ceili dancing, step dancing, and set dancing to
         traditional music including fiddle, flute, tin
         whistle, pipes, fife and drum bands, voice, and pipe
         bands. Also competition in crafts: needlecrafts,
         painting, crochet, embroidery, industrial arts--all
         with Irish themes.

         Dates: June .
         Open to the public. Audience size: 4,000.
         Information on photographs not available.

                              +++++

OH157   IRISH CULTURAL FESTIVAL OF CLEVELAND

         Parma

OH157   (Irish Cultural Festival of Cleveland)
cont.
         John O'Brien
         14708 Westland Avenue
         Cleveland, OH   44111
         (216) 251-0711

         This festival started in 1983. Includes a football
         tournament, a lace maker from Ireland, local dancing
         schools, and local and international dancers and
         musicians. Also has a storyteller from Ireland,
         Mass, food, and a cultural gallery. Proceeds go to
         Project Children, which brings children from
         Northern Ireland to the United States, and also to
         students of Irish music.

         Dates: 1st weekend in August.
         Open to the public. Audience: 7-8,000.
         Photographs available to researchers.

                            +++++

PA158   IRISH JUBILEE AND CELTIC FESTIVAL

         Rocky Glen Park
         Moosic, PA

         Rocky Glen Park
         P.O. Box 37
         Avoca, PA 18641-0037
         (717) 451-7401

         Sponsor: Rocky Glen Park

         Festival is held at amuseument park. Began in 1983,
         includes step dancing, music, crafts, food, and a
         Mass. Also amusement rides.

         Dates: August.
         Open to the public.
         No photographs available to researchers.

                            +++++

PA159   IRISH CENTRE OF PITTSBURGH FEIS

         Irish Centre of Pittsburgh

         Patsy Shovlin
         6886 Forward Avenue
         Pittsburgh, PA   15217
         (412) 521-9712

         Sponsor: Irish Centre of Pittsbugh

         Feis began in 1968. Participants come from the
         Northeast, Mid-west, and Canada for dancing
         competition.
                             Ohio-Pennsylvania (Festivals)

PA159   (Irish Centre of Pittsburgh Feis)
cont.
          Dates: 3rd Saturday of July.
          Open to the public. Audience: 400-600.
          No photographs available to researchers.

                         +++++

PA160   IRISH FESTIVAL AT JACK FROST MOUNTAIN

          Pocono Mountains

          Jerry Clark
          P.O. Box 573
          Scranton, PA   18501
          (717) 961-0143

          Sponsor: Irish Cultural Society

          Festival began in 1985. Formerly held at Montage
          Mountain, now in the Poconos. Includes children's
          step dancing, adult step dancing, ceili dancing.
          Also local and international musicians, crafts,
          and food. Mass is held on Sunday at noon.

          Dates: Memorial Day weekend.
          Open to the public. Audience: 5,000.
          Photographs available to researchers.

                         +++++

PA161   IRISH DAYS

          Coal Street Park

          George Horn
          42 Maxwell Street
          Wilkes-Barre, PA   18702
          (717) 822-7376

          Sponsor: The Donegal Society

          Festival started in 1980 by the Donegal Society to
          support local ceili dancers who wanted to go to a
          competition. Most groups from Wilkes-Barre but also
          includes groups from Philadelphia area, upstate New
          York, and Ireland. Mass on Sunday. Includes
          step dancing demonstrations, bagpipe bands, music,
          Irish food, and sports.

          Dates: Weekend following the 4th of July.
          Open to the public. Audience: 10,000+.
          Photographs available to researchers.

                         +++++

TX162   NORTH TEXAS IRISH FEST

         Fair Park

         Ken Fleming
         P.O. Box 4474
         Dallas, TX   75208
         (214) 942-6687

         Began in 1983,this festival is held on the state
         fair grounds and is organized by the Southwest
         Celtic Music Association. Festival first began as a

         ceili, now includes local, regional, national, and
         international performers. Music and dance
         workshops, children's fair, traditional Irish foods,
         crafts, Mass.

         Dates: 1st weekend in March
         Open to the public. Audience: 12,000 in 1986.
         Photographs available to researchers.

                              +++++

TX163   TEXAS IRISH FESTIVAL

         La Villita Plaza

         Tom Harrell
         St. Mary's Church
         202 North Saint Mary's Street
         San Antonio, TX   78205
         (512) 226-8381

         Sponsor: 30 community organizations

         This festival is in its 4th year and is a
         multi-ethnic event. Proceeds for the benefit of
         St. Mary's Catholic Church. Includes local bands
         and step dancers, bagpipers, food, and a Mass. Also
         includes a Chinese lion dance and country-western
         music.

         Dates: Weekend before St. Patrick's Day.
         Open to the public. Audience: 25-30,000.
         Photographs available to researchers.

                              +++++

WI164   MILWAUKEE IRISH FEST

         Summerfest Grounds

         Martin Hintz
         P.O. Box 599
         Milwaukee, WI   53201
         (414) 963-4522

WI164   (Milwaukee Irish Fest)
cont.
         Sponsor: Irish Fest Board

         Started in 1980, this festival was created to
         advance Irish music and culture, and to establish an
         Irish cultural center in Milwaukee. One of the
         largest Irish festivals in the United States, it
         includes national, international, and local dancers
         and musicians. Also has the O'Darby Irish Fest
         Theater, children's programs, gaelic football,
         hurling matches, Sunday morning Mass, and a cultural
         tent.

         Dates: 3rd weekend in August.
         Open to the public. Audience: 79,100.
         Photographs, video, and audio tapes available to
         researchers.

                         +++++

NB165   CANADA'S IRISH FESTIVAL ON THE MIRAMICHI

         Chatham, New Brunswick

         Farrell McCarthy
         109 Roy Avenue
         Newcastle, New Brunswick, EIV 3N8
         (506) 622-4007

         Sponsor: Irish Canadian Cultural Association of
                  New Brunswick

         This festival began as small community festival in
         1983. It now draws people from the Maritime
         Provinces as well as the United States. Includes
         pipe bands, step dancing, ceili dancing, and local,
         regional, and international performers. Also has an
         Irish restaurant, Irish plays, an Irish art gallery,
         fashion show, crafts,and a Mass on Sunday.

         Dates: 3rd weekend in July.
         Open to the public. Audience: 15,000.
         Photographs available to researchers.

                         +++++

Selected List of Irish Sources

BELCARAA FOLK MUSEUM
Belacarra, Castlebar
County Mayo
Ireland

Folklife, pictures of the Famine.

                        +++++

BUNRATTY CASTLE AND FOLK PARK
Bunratty
County Clare
Ireland
(061) 61511

Furniture, tapestries and works of art, folklife, dwelling
houses, outhouses and craft workshops. Also exhibition of
agricultural machines.

                        +++++

CASTLERUDDERY TRANSPORT MUSEUM
Donard
County Wicklow
Ireland
(01) 311130

Folklife, industrial archaeology.

                        +++++

CORK PUBLIC MUSEUM
Fitzgerald Park
Cork
Ireland
(021) 20679

National, local and social history; archaeology.

                        +++++

COUNTY CARLOW MUSEUM
Town Hall
Carlow
Ireland
(0503) 31759

Folklife, archaeology, natural history.

                              +++++

COUNTY MUSEUM (THE CASTLE)
Castle Street
Enniscorthy
County Wexford
Ireland

Folklife, archaeology.

                              +++++

CRAGGAUNOWEN PROJECT
Quin
County Clare
Ireland
(061) 72178

Full-scale model of crannog (Bronze Age lake dwelling). The
"Brendan," a hide boat sailed from Ireland to America by Tim
Severin, on display.

                              +++++

DE VALERA LIBRARY AND MUSEUM
Harmony Row
Ennis
County Clare
Ireland
(065) 21616

Paintings, archaeology, history.

                              ++++++

FOLK MUSEUM
Toomevara
County Tipperay
Ireland

19th and 20th century rural exhibits.

                              +++++

MONAGHAN COUNTY MUSEUM
The Courthouse
Monaghan
Ireland
(047) 82211

(Monaghan County Musem cont.)
Archaeology, folklife, local history, crafts, lace.

+++++

FOLK MUSEUM
MUCKROSS HOUSE
Killarney
County Kerry
Ireland
(064) 31440

Folklife.

+++++

NATIONAL GALLERY OF IRELAND
Merrion Square West
Dublin 2
Ireland
(01) 608533
Janet Drew, Director's P.A.

Photos: art. Collection includes Irish-American artists.

+++++

NATIONAL LIBRARY
Kildare Street
Dublin 2
Ireland
(01) 765521
Michael Hewson, Director

Collection includes photos, manuscripts, broadsides.
Irish-American materials not separately treated but
available.

+++++

NATIONAL MUSEUM
Kildare Street
Dublin 2
Ireland
01-765521
Felicity Devlin, Librarian

Collection related to Irish-American materials includes
weapons, broadsides, letters, fraternal items.
Military/historical collections.

+++++

SLIGO COUNTY MUSEUM
Stephen Street
Sligo
Ireland
(071) 2212

(Sligo County Museum cont.)
Folklife, archaeology, history, paintings, rare printed
books, manuscripts. Items relating to J. B. Yeats.

+++++

TRIM MUSEUM
Trim
County Meath
Ireland

Archaeology, folklife, and history.

+++++

ULSTER AMERICAN FOLK PARK
Mellon Road
Castletown, Omagh
County Tyrone
Northern Ireland BT78 5QY
Dr. Denis MacNeice, Director

Large collection of Irish and Irish American materials
including buildings, bedding, furniture, lighting devices,
clothing, personal adornments, luggage, toilet articles,
agricultural tools, weapons, food processing, housekeeping
tools, musical instruments, textile tools, clocks,
woodworking tools, pottery, transportation, advertising
media, religious objects, containers, diaries. Photos:
agriculture, clothing, communication, customs and
celebrations, education, hotels, inns, household interiors,
industry, military, neighborhoods, occupations, people,
structures, transportation.

+++++

ULSTER FOLK AND TRANSPORT MUSEUM
Cultra Manor, Holywood
County Down
Northern Ireland BT 18 OEU
Dr. W. H. Crawford, Keeper of Material Culture
Staff: 25 graduates

Collection includes photos, objects, historic buildings,
oral history. 18-building complex which studies and
represents life and traditions in Northern Ireland.
Irish-American materials in library.

+++++

WEST CORK REGIONAL MUSEUM
Old Methodist School
Western Road
Clonakilty
County Cork
Ireland

Folklife and history of the region.
+++++

Bibliography

History

Akenson, Donald Harmen. <u>Being Had: Historians, Evidence and the Irish in North America</u>. Ontario: P.D. Meany, 1984.

Blessing, Patrick. "Irish." <u>Harvard Encyclopedia of Ethnic Groups</u>. Cambridge, MA: Harvard University Press, 1980. Pp.524-545.

Callwood, June. <u>Portrait of Canada</u>. Garden City, NY: Doubleday and Company, 1981.

Clark, Dennis. <u>Hibernia America: The Irish and Regional Cultures</u>. Westport CT: Greenwood Press, 1986.

Clark, Dennis. <u>The Irish in Philadelphia: Ten Generations of Urban Experience</u>. Philadelphia: Temple University Press, 1981.

Doyle, David. <u>Ireland, Irishmen and Revolutionary America 1760-1820</u>. Cork, Ireland: The Mercier Press, 1981.

Diner, Hasia R. <u>Erin's Daughters in America: Irish Immigrant Women in the 19th Century</u>. Baltimore: The John Hopkins University Press, 1983.

Eid, Leroy V. "The Colonial Scotch-Irish: A View Accepted Too Readily." <u>Eire-Ireland</u>, Winter, 1986, Pp. 81-105.

Fallows, Marjorie R. <u>Irish Americans: Identity and Assimilation</u>. Englewood Cliffs NJ: Prentice-Hall, 1979.

Funchion, Michael F., ed. <u>Irish American Voluntary Organizations</u>. Westport CT: Greenwood Press, 1983.

Greeley, Andrew M. That Most Distressful Nation, The
Taming of the American Irish. Chicago: Quadrangle Books,
1972.

Jones, Maldwyn A. "Scotch-Irish." Harvard
Encyclopedia Of Ethnic Groups. Cambridge: Harvard
University Press, 1984. Pp. 895-906.

Leyburn, J.G. The Scotch-Irish. Chapel Hill:
University of North Carolina Press, 1962.

McCaffrey, Lawrence J. The Irish Diaspora in North
America. Bloomington: Indiana University Press, 1976.

McCaffrey, Lawrence J., Ellen Skerrett, Michael
Funchion, and Charles Fanning. The Irish in Chicago.
Chicago: University of Illinois Press, 1987.

Miller, Kerby A. Emigrants and Exiles: Ireland and
the Irish Exodus to North America. New York: Oxford
University Press, 1985 .

Neidhart, W.S. Fenianism in North America.
University Park: Penn State University Press, 1975.

Ridge, John T. Erin's Sons in America: The Ancient
Order of Hibernians. New York: AOH Publications, 1986.

Ryan, Dennis P. Beyond the Ballot Box: A Social
History of the Boston Irish 1845-1917. East Brunswick, NJ:
Associated University Press, 1983.

Shannon, William V. The American Irish: A Political
And Social Portrait. New York: Collier MacMillian
Publishers, 1974.

Wittke, Carl. The Irish in America. Baton Rouge:
Louisiana State University Press, 1956.

Material Culture

Concannon, John, and Frank Cull. The Irish
Directory. Pearl River, NY: P.O. Box 735, 1983.

Cooper, Brian E., ed. The Irish-American Almanac and
Green Pages. New York: Pembroke Press, 1986.

DeBreffny, Brian, ed. Ireland: A Cultural
Encylopedia. New York: Facts on File, 1983.

Evans, E. Estyn. Irish Folk Ways. London:
Routledge and Kegan Paul Ltd., 1957.

Fitz-gerald, Desmond. "Irish Furniture and Its
Influence on Philadelphia 1720-1750." Program guide to
Philadelphia's Irish Legacy, 1984 Antiques Show.
Philadelphia: Hospital of the University of Pennsylvania,
1984.

Glassie, Henry. Passing the Time in Ballymenone,
Culture and History of an Ulster Community. Philadelphia:
University of Pennsylvania Press, 1982.

Gribben, Arthur and Marsha Maguire. The Irish
Cultural Directory for Southern California. Los Angeles:
UCLA Folklore and Mythology Publications, 1985.

Griffin, William D. A Portrait of the Irish in
America. New York: Charles Scribner's and Sons, 1981.

Guide to the Boston Irish. Boston: Quinlan
Campbell, 1985.

Guide to the New England Irish. Boston: Quinlan
Campbell, 1987.

Lane, George, A.S.J. Chicago Churches and
Synagogues, An Architectural Pilgrimage. Chicago:
Loyola U. Press, 1981.

Mannion, John J. Irish Settlements in Eastern
Canada, A Study of Cultural Transfer and Adaptation.
Toronto: University of Toronto Press, 1974.

Ireland: Museums and Libraries. Information Sheet
No. 5. Dublin: Irish Tourist Board-Bord Failte, 1984.

Neill, Susan. O'Neill's Pocket Guide to Irish New
York. New York: Five Points Press, 1983.

Raley, R. L. "Irish Influences in Baltimore Decorative
Arts 1785-1815." Antiques, March 1961, Pp. 276-279.

Reilly, A. J. Irish Landmarks in New York.
Worchester: Harrigan Press, Inc., 1939.

Rogers, Meyric R. "Philadelphia via Dublin: Influences
in Rococo Furniture." Antiques, March, 1961, Pp.
272-275.

Sharkey, Olive. Old Days and Old Ways, An
Illustrated Folk History of Ireland. Dublin: The O'Brien
Press, 1985.

Stockwell, David. "Irish Influence in Pennsylvania
Queen Anne Furniture." Antiques, March, 1961, Pp.
269-271.

Reference Works

Archival and Manuscript Repositories in Metropolitan
Chicago and the Calumet Region of Northwest Indiana.
Chicago: Chicago Area Archivists, 1986.

Ash, Lee. Subject Collections. New York: R. R.
Bowker, 1985

Chenhall, R. G. Nomenclature for Museum Cataloging:
A System for Classifying Man-Made Objects. Nashville:
American Association for State and Local History, 1978.

Directory of Historical Societies and Agencies in the
United States and Canada. Thirteenth Edition. Nashville:
American Association for State and Local History, 1986.

Encyclopedia of Assocations. Detroit: Gale Research,
1976.

Griffin, W. D. The Irish in America 550-1972, A
Chronology and Fact Book. Doffs Ferry, NY: Oceana
Publications, 1973.

Metress, S. P. Irish-American Experience, A
Bibliography. Washington, DC: University Press of America,
1981.

The National Register of Historic Places. Washington,
DC: U. S. Department of the Interior, 1976.

The Official Museum Directory, 1985-86. Washington,
DC:
American Association of Museums, 1986.

Shaw, R. V. Picture Searching: Techniques and
Tools. New York: Special Libraries Association, 1973.

Wasserman, P. and Alice Kennington, eds. Ethnic
Information Sources of the United States. Second Edition.
Detroit: Gale Research Company, 1983.

The World of Learning. 36th Edition. London: Europa
Publications, Ltd., 1986.

Wynar, Lubomyr. Encyclopedic Directory of Ethnic
Organizations in the United States. Littleton, CO:
Libraries Unlimited, 1975.

Wynar, Lubomyr and Lois Buttlar, eds. Guide to
Ethnic Museums, Libraries and Archives in the United
States. Kent, Ohio: Center for Ethnic Publications, 1978.

Name Index

American Irish Historical Society	NY55
American Museum of Immigration	NY56
Ancient Order of Hibernians	MA35
------- Albany Chapter	NY52
Annual Feis	DE142
Appel, John and Selma	MI42
Archdiocese of Boston	MA33
Archdiocese of Chicago	IL13
Austin Historic District	NV111
Balch Institute for Ethnic Studies, The	PA68
Baltimore City Life Museums	MD26
Baltimore Irish Festival	MD145
Bettman Archive	NY57
Boston Athenaeum	MA27
Boston College	MA34
Boston Public Library	MA28
Bostonian Society, The	MA29
Brandywine Manufacturers' Sunday School	DE95
Buffalo Irish Festival	NY153
California Historical Society	CA1

Camden County Historical Society   NJ50

Canada's Irish Festival on the Miramichi   NB165

Carroll Mansion   MD105

Catholic University of America Library   DC9

Cato Hill Historic Disctrict   RI129

Celtic Cross   NB135

Celtic Cross-Quebec   QU137

Chemung County Historical Society   NY54

Chicago Historical Society   IL14

Chicago Public Library   IL15

Church of St. Bridget   MN110

College of St. Rose, The   NY53

College of the Holy Cross   MA38

Connecticut Historical Society   CT5

Daniel Boone Homestead Site   PA120

Dean Family Farm   OH117

Denver Public Library   CO4

Detroit Institute of Arts   MI40

Detroit Public Library   MI41

Dobbin House   PA122

Eckley Miner's Village   PA74

Eleutherian Mills   DE96

Empire State Festival   NY151

Eugene V. Kelly Carriage House   NJ112

Felix Grimes House   KY101

Feodar Protar Cabin   MI109

Fisher's Paradise   DE94

Fitchburg Irish Festival   MA146

Florida Folklife Program   FL12

Georgetown University Astronomical Observatory   DC98

Gettysburg Battlefield Historic District   PA123

Grand National Irish Fair and Music Festival   CA139

Great Conewago Presbyterian Church   PA124

Greeneville Historic District   TN131

Guinston United Presbyterian Church   PA125

Hagley Museum and Library   DE6

Greater Hartford Irish Festival   CT141

Hibernian Hall   SC130

Hibernian Society of Charleston, South Carolina   SC76

Historical Society of Delaware   DE7

Historical Society of Pennsylvania   PA69

Historical Society of Princeton   NJ51

Historic Murphy's Landing   MN44

Historic New Orleans Collection   LA24

Holy Name High School   OH116

(Former) Immaculate Conception Church   RI128

Immigrant City Archives   MA36

Indiana State Museum   IN21

Institute of Texan Cultures   TX78

International Celtic Festival   NY154

International House   PA70

Irish American Cultural Center of New York   NY54A

Irish American Heritage Center   IL16

Irish Centre of Pittsburgh   PA73

-------------------------Feis   PA159

Irish Cultural Festival of Cleveland   OH157

Irish Days   PA161

Irish Fest   IL143

Irish Festival   NJ150

Irish Festival at Jack Frost Mountain   PA160

Irish Festival of Detroit   MI148

Irish Heritage Weekend   KY144

Irish Jubilee and Celtic Festival   PA158

Irish Music Festival   NY155

James C. Flood Mansion   CA92

James H. McBirney House   OK118

James McGloin Homestead   TX132

James Miller House   PA119

Jeramiah Curtin House   WI134

Kansas State Historical Society   KS23

Library Company of Philadelphia   PA71

Library of Congress   DC11

Long's Peak Scottish Highlands Festival   CO140

Loyola University of Chicago   IL17

Massachusetts Historical Society   MA30

Memorial University of Newfoundland   NF86

Metropolitan Museum of Art   NY58

Milwaukee County Historical Society   WI84

Milwaukee Irish Fest   WI164

Milwaukee Public Museum   WI85

Minnesota Historical Society   MN45

Minnesota Irish Festival   MN149

Missouri Historical Society   MO46

Molly Brown House   CO93

Museum and Library of Maryland History   MD25

Museum of American Textile History   MA37

Museum of Fine Arts   MA31

Museum of the City of New York	NY59
National Museum of Man	ON88
Nebraska State Historical Society	NE47
Nevada Historical Society	NV49
New England Irish Festival	MA147
New Melleray Abbey	IA22
New York City Fire Museum	NY60
New York Historical Society	NY61
New York Public Library	NY62
Nicholas Newlin House	PA121
North Texas Irish Fest	TX162
Obelisk of Honor	PA127
Old Roman Catholic Cathedral	MD106
Old World Wisconsin	WI82
Oregon Historical Society	OR67
Philadelphia Museum of Art	PA72
Phoenix Irish Feis	AZ138
Prince Edward Island Museum and Heritage Foundation	PEI90
Providence Public Library	RI75
Provincial Archives of Newfoundland and Labrador	NF87
Public Archives Canada	ON89
Rensselaer County Historical Society	NY64
Ridgeway Battlefield	ON136
Sisters of Mercy Province Center	IL18
Sloan-Parker House	WV133
Smithsonian Institution	DC10
Society for the Preservation of New England Antiquities	MA32
Society of California Pioneers	CA3
Southern Appalachian Historical Association	NC65

St. Alphonsus Church   LA102

St. Augustine's Catholic Church   PA126

St. Denis Catholic Church   ME104

St. Francis Xavier Church   MD107

St. James Church   NY113

St. John's Catholic Church   ME103

St. Joseph's on the Brandywine   DE97

St. Joseph Roman Catholic Church   KY100

St. Mary's Church   TX79

St. Patrick's Cathedral   NY114

St. Patrick Church   IL99

St. Stephen's Church   MA108

State Historical Society of Wisconsin   WI83

Staten Island Historical Society   NY63

Tennessee State Museum   TN77

Texas Irish Festival   TX163

The Great Irish Fair   NY152

Union Pacific Railroad Museum   NE46

Union Street Historic District   NY115

United Irish Counties Association Feis   NY156

United Irish Cultural Center   CA2

University of Illinois at Chicago   IL19

University of Minnesota-Morris   MN43

Valentine Museum   VA80

Valley Creek Presbyterian Church   AL91

West Chicago Historical Museum   IL20

Western Reserve Historical Society   OH66

West Virginia State Museum and Archives   WV81

Winterthur Museum Library   DE8

Worcester Historical Museum   MA39

General Index

The terms used in this index may be broken down into
the following categories: articles of material culture
(furniture, tools, buildings, etc.); subjects of historical
photographs (occupations, customs and celebrations, people,
etc.); events at Irish-American festivals (crafts, food,
costume, religious services); and general events in
Irish-American history such as the Famine.

The terms applied to articles of material culture are
mostly drawn from Robert G. Chenall's Nomenclature for
Museum Cataloging. Terms relevant or unique to
Irish-Americana have been added where needed. Subject
categories for the most part are broad, although specific
listings have been made for unusual items, such as sod from
Ireland. The purpose of this book is to give an overview of
material culture of Irish-Americans and Irish-Canadians and
to facilitate more detailed research in specific areas.

Terms for photographs are drawn from an article by
Margaret Hobbie on cataloging historical photographs which
was issued by the Regional Conference of Historical Agencies
in 1981. Terms for festivals were suggested by an article
by Beverly J. Stoeltje in Handbook of American Folklore
(1983) by Richard M. Dorson.

The entries for museum collections (CA1-PE90), National
Register Sites (AL91-QU137), and festivals (AZ138-NB165) are
arranged in numerical order. Letter codes indicating state
or province have been prefixed to each entry number to help
the user discern the geographical location of the collection
or site. These letter codes are explained below.

Listings marked with an asterisk indicate photographs,
other categories are objects, historical terms, or festival
categories.

EXPLANATION OF LETTER CODES

Alabama	AL	Minnesota	MN
Arizona	AZ	Missouri	MO
California	CA	Nebraska	NE
Colorado	CO	New Jersey	NJ
Connecticut	CT	New York	NY
Delaware	DE	Nevada	NV
Washington, D.C.	DC	Ohio	OH
Florida	FL	Oklahoma	OK
Ilinois	IL	Pennsylvania	PA
Indiana	IN	Rhode Island	RI
Kansas	KS	South Carolina	SC
Kentucky	KY	Tennessee	TN
Maine	ME	Texas	TX
Maryland	MD	Virginia	VA
Massachusetts	MA	West Virginia	WV
Michigan	MI	Wisconsin	WI

New Brunswick	NB	Quebec	QU
Newfoundland	NF	Prince Edward Island	PE
Ontario	ON		

Achora (rowboats), MD145

Advertisements*, DE8,
  LA24, MD26, MA28, MA29,
  MA32, MA36, MA39, MI42,
  PA71, PA73

Advertising media, DC11,
  LA24, MD26, MA29, MA36,
  MA39, MI42, NY64, PA73,
  PE90

Agricultural tools, WI83

Agriculture*, DE8, LA24,
  MA32, TX78

Alabama, AL91

Ancient Order of Hibernians,
  CA2, MA34, MA35, NV49,
  NY52, TX79, PE90, NY113,
  PA127, NY152

Animals*, DE8, MA32

Appalachians, NC65

Arizona, AZ138

Art*, CA2, DE7, DE8,
  IL14, Il16, Il18, IL19,
  LA24, MD25, MA28, MA29,
  MA32, MA33, MA34, MI40,
  MN45, MO46, NY55, NY60,
  NY62, PA69, PA71, PA73,
  SC76,TN77, WI82, WI83,
  WI85, PE90

Art objects, CA2, DE7, DE8,
  IL14, IL16, IL18, IL19,
  LA24, MA28, MA29, MA33,
  MA34, MI40, MO46, NY55,
  NY56, NY60, NY62, PA69,
  PA71, PA72, PA73, SC76,
  TN77, WI85

Bagpipges, NY150, NY151,
  PA161, TX163

Baltimore, MD26, MD105,
  MD106, MD145

Banners, CA2

Bedding, MA29, NE47, PA68,
  WI83

Boston, MA27, MA28, MA29,
  MA30, MA31, MA32, MA33,
  MA34, MA108

Broadsides, CA1, DE6, DC11,
  IL14, IL15, IL19, LA24,
  MD26, MA29, MA34, NE47,
  NY61, NY62, PA68, PA71,
  PA74, RI75, WI83

Buildings (actual structure)
  See also: Churches
            Farms
            Houses
            Log Barn
            Log Cabin
            Mills
            Stores
  AL91, CA92, CO93, DE94,
  DE95, DE96, DE97, DC98,
  IL99, KY100, KY101,
  LA102, ME103, ME104,
  MD105, MD106, MA107,
  MA108, MI109, MN110,
  NV111, NJ112, NY113,
  NY114, NY115, OH116,
  OH117, OK118, PA119,
  PA120, PA121, PA122,
  PA124, PA125, PA126,
  RI128, RI129, SC130,
  TN131, TX132, WV133,
  WI134

Busts, CA2

California, CA1, CA2, CA3
  CA92, CA139

Canada, NF86, NF87, ON88,
  ON89, PE90, NB135, ON136,
  QU137, CO140, DE142,
  NY153, NB165

Canes, WI83

Caricatures, MI42, NY61,
  NY62, PA68

Catholics, DC9, IL17, MA32,
  MA33, MA34, MA38, DE97,
  DC98, IL99, KY100, LA102,
  ME103, ME104, MD107,
  MA108, MN110, OH116,
  PA126, RI128

Cattlebrands, TX78

Ceili, MD145, MNI49, NY155,
  NY156, PA160

Chicago, IL13, IL14, IL15,
    IL16, IL18, IL99

Children, CO140, CT141,
    IL143, MA147, NY152,
    OH157, PA158, PA160,
    TX162, WI164

Churches, DE6, ME103,
    MD106, MA108, MN110,
    NV111, NY113, NY114,
    PA126, RI128

Civil War, PA123, PA127,
    AZ138

Cleveland, OH116

Clocks, MA29, NE47, NY55

Clothing*, DE6, DE8,
    IL14, IL18, LA24, MA29,
    MA32, MA33, MN45, NE47,
    NY64, PA68, TX78, WI82,
    WI83, PE90

Clubs and organizations*,
    CA2, DE8, IL15, LA24, MA29,
    MA32, MA33, MA36, MA38,
    MA39, NY61, NY64, TX79

Coins, CA2, MI40

Colonization, MN110

Colorado, CO4, CO140

Costumes, CA139, MN149

Communication*, DE8,
    LA24

Connecticut, CT5, CT141

Containers, MA29, MI40,
    MN45, NY56, WI83, WI85

Crafts, DC11, MA29, AZ138,
    CA139, CO140, CT141,
    DE142, IL143, KY144,
    MD145, MA146, MI148,
    MN149, NY151, NY152,
    NY153, NY154, NY155,
    NY156, OH157, PA158,
    PA160, TX162, NB165

Criminals and crime, DE8,
    LA24, NY62, PA74

Customs and celebrations,
    CA2, DE6, DE8, DC11,
    IL14, IL16, IL19, LA24,
    MD26, MA29, MA32, MA33,
    MA36, NY61, PA68, PA73,
    TX78, WI85

Daily Life, CA1

Dance
    See also: Step dance
                Ceili
    DC11, AZ138, CA139,
    CO140, CT141, DE142,
    IL143, KY144, MD145,
    MA146, MA147, MI148,
    MN149, NJ150, NY151,
    NY152, NY153, NY154,
    NY155, NY156, OH157,
    PA158, PA159, PA160,
    PA161, TX162, TX163,
    WI164, NB165

Delaware, DE6, DE7, DE8,
    DE94, DE95, DE96, DE97,
    DE142

Detroit, MI141, MI148

Diaries, CA1< IL19, LA24,
    MA29, MA33, MA36, NY61,
    OH66, WI84

Disasters*, LA24, MA29,
    MA32, MA36, NY60, WI84,
    ON89

Door from ship, WI84

Education*, DE6, DE8,
    IL18, LA24, MA29, MA32,
    MA33, MA36, NY64, TX78

Entertainment*, DE8,
    DC11, IL16, LA24, MA32,
    PA68, PA70, WI85, ON89

Exhibit, CT5, IL16, IL19,
    NJ50, NY61, PA68, PA74,
    TX78, WI82, WI85, AXZ138,
    CT141, IL143, KY144,
    MI148, NJ150, WI164

Famine, ON89, NY113, NB135,
    WU137

Farmers, ON89

Farms, OH117

Feisanna, AZ138, DE142,
  NY156, PA159

Fenians, NV49, ON136

Festivals, CA139, CT141,
  DE142, IL143, KY144,
  MA146, MA147, MN149,
  NY151, NY153, NY155

Fire fighting, NY60

Fishing, hunting, and
  trapping, LA24, MA32

Florida, FL12

Food, CA139, CO140, CT141,
  IL143, KY144, MD145,
  MA147, NJ150, NY151,
  NY152, NY153, NY154,
  NY155, PA158, PA160,
  PA161, TX163, NB165

Food processing and service
  articles, DE6, MD25, MA29,
  PA72, TN77, PE90

Foodways*, DE8, LA24,
  MA29, MA32, ON89

Furniture, DE8, IL14, MA29,
  MI40, NY55, NY58, PA69,
  PA72, WI82, WI85

Fraternal and social
  organization items, CA2,
  IL14, IL15, IL16, LA24,
  MD26, MA29, MA33, MA34,
  MA35, MA39, MI40, NY55,
  NY64, PA73, PA74, WI83,
  PE90

Gaelic football, AZ138,
  NJ150, OH157

Games, MA29, NY154

Gettysburg, PA123

Government*, CA1, CA2,
  DE8, LA24, PA68

Gravestones, TX78

Halls, SC130

Health and medicine*,
  DE8, LA24, MA29, MA32

Hotels, Taverns, Inns*,
  DE6, DE8, DC11, LA24,
  MD26, MA29, MA32, MA36,
  TX78

Household interiors*,
  DE6, DE8, DC11, LA24,
  MA29, MA32, WI85

Housekeeping tools, MA29,
  WI82, WI85

Houses, KY101, MD105,
  MI109, NV111, NJ112,
  OH117, OK118, TN131,
  TX132, WV133

Illinois, IL14, IL15, IL16,
  IL19, IL20, IL99, IL143

Immigrants, DE6, IL18,
  IL19, IA22, TX78, ON89,
  CO93, DE95, DE96, DE97,
  KY101, ME104, MI109,
  MN110, NV111, NJ112,
  NY113, NY115, OH117,
  OK118, PA119, RI129,
  SC130, WV133, NB135,
  QU137

Immigration, NY56, NY61,
  ON89

Indiana, IN21

Industry and Commerce*,
  DE6, IL20, MA29, MA36,
  MA39, NY64, PA68, TX78

Kansas, KS23

Kentucky, KY100, KY101,
  KY144

Letter opener, WI83

Lighting devices, MA29,
  WI82

Log barn, WV133

Log cabin, MI109

Louisiana, LA102

Luggage, DE6, IL19, MA29,
  MN45, WI82, WI83

Maine, ME103, ME104

Maps, MN43, PA69

Marine, MA29

Maryland, MD25, MD26,
  MD106, MD107, MD145

Massachusetts, MA27, MA28,
  MA29, MA30, MA32, MA33,
  MA34, MA35, MA36, MA39,
  MA146, MA147

Michigan, MI40, MI41, MI42,
  MI148

Memorials, ON89

Military*, DE8, IL14,
  LA24, MA29, MA32, MA38,
  NY55, NY61, NY64, TX78,
  ON89, PA127, ON136

Mills, DE96

Mill tools, NY63

Milwaukee, WI84, WI164

Miners, PA74, CA92, KY101

Mining, PA74, CO93, NV111

Minnesota, MN43, MN44,
  MN45, MN149

Missouri, MO46

Montana, DC11

Monuments, PA123, PA127,
  NB135, ON136, QU137

Mummers' masks, NF86

Music*, DE6, DE8, DC10,
  IL16, IN21, LA24, MA29,
  MA32, MA33, NY55, NY56,
  PA58, PA70, PA73, RI75,
  TX78, WI85, PE90, CA139,
  CO140, CT141, DE142,
  IL143, KY144, MD145,
  MA146, MA147, MI148,
  MN149, NJ150, NY151,

(Music)
  NY152, NY153, NY154,
  NY155, NY156, OH157,
  PA158, PA160, PA161,
  TX162, TX163, WI164,
  NB165

Musical instruments, DE6,
  IL16, IN21, MA29, NY55,
  PA73, WI85

Music and dancing, PA68

Nature*, DE8, LA24,
  MA29

Nebraska, NE47

Needlepoint hangings, CA2,
  IL16

Neighborhoods*, CA1,
  DE8, IL15, IL19, LA24,
  MA29, MA32, MA33, MA36,
  NY62, PA68, TX78, NY115,
  RI129

Nevada, NV49, NV111

New Brunswick, NB135, NB165

New Foundland, NF86, NF87

New Jersey, NJ50, NJ51,
  NJ112, NJ150

New Orleans, LA24, LA102

New York, IN21, MI40, NY52,
  NY53, NY54, NY55, NY55A,
  NY59, NY60, NY61, NY62,
  NY63, NY113, NY114,
  NY115, NY152, NY153,
  NY154, NY155

New York City, NY55A, NY62,
  NY113

North Carolina, NC65, AL91

Objects, CA2, CT5, DE7,
  DE8, DC9, IL14, IL15,
  IL16, IL18, IL19, IA22,
  LA24, MA28, MA29, MA30,
  MA33, MA34, MI40, MN44,
  MO46, NJ50, NY53, NY54,
  NY55, NY55A, NY56, NY60,
  NY62, NY64, OR67, PA69,
  PA71, PA72, PA73, PA74,

(Objects)
SC76, TN77, VA80, WI82,
WI85, ON88

Occupations*, CA1, DE6,
DE8, IL15, IL20, MA28,
MA29, MA37, NE48, NY60,
NY62, OH66, PA68, PA74,
TX78, WI83

Ohio, OH66, OH116, OH157

Oklahoma, OK118

Ontario, ON88, ON89, ON136

Oral history, CO4, DE8,
DC10, DC11, MA36, MA38,
MN43, MN45, NJ50, NY56,
NY63, OR67, PA68, PA70,
PA73, TX78, WI83, NF86,
ON88

Oregon, OR67

Pamphlets, MA39, RI75

Pennsylvania, PA68, PA70,
PA73, PA74, PA110, PA120,
PA121, PA122, PA123,
PA124, PA125, PA126,
PA127, PA158, PA160, PA161

People*, CA1, CA2, DE6,
DE8, DC11, IL14, IL15,
IL16, IL17, IL18, IL19,
IL20, LA24, MA28, MA29,
MA32, MA33, MA35, MA36,
MA38, MA39, MN45, NY55,
NY56, NY60, NY62, PA68,
PA69, TX78, WI83, WI84,
WI85, ON89

Personal adornments, DE6,
DE7, MA29, MA33, MN45,
NY56, PA68, PA74, WI82,
PE90

Philadelphia, DE8, PA68,
PA69, PA70, PA71, PA126

Photos*, CA1, CA2, CA3,
CO4, CT5, DE6, DE7, DE8,
DC9, DC10, DC11, IL13,
IL14, IL15, IL16, IL17,
IL18, IL19, IL20, KS23,
LA24, MD26, MA27, MA28,
MA29, MA30, MA32, MA33,

(Photos)
MA35, MA36, MA37, MA38,
MA39, MI40, MI41, MI42,
MN44, MN45, MO46, NE48,
NJ51, NY52, NY53, NY54,
NY55, NY55A, NY56, NY57,
NY59, NY60, NY61, NY62,
NY63, NY64, OH66, OR67,
PA69, PA70, PA71, PA73,
PA74, SC76, TX78, TX79,
VA80, WV81, WI83, WI84,
WI85, NF86, NF87, ON88,
ON89, AZ138, CA139,
CO140, DE142, IL143,
KY144, MA146, MA147,
MI148, MN149, NJ150,
NY151, NY152, NY154,
OH157, PA160, PA161,
TX162, TX163, WI164,
NB165

Pittsburgh, PA73

Politics*, CA1, CA2,
DE8, DC11, IL14, IL15,
IL16, LA24, MD26, MA28,
MA29, MA32, MA33, MA36,
NY55, NY62, TX78, SC130

Postcards, IL18

Posters, CA1

Pottery, IL16, MA29, MA31,
MA34, MI40, NY55, NY56,
PA73, WI85, PE90

Presbyterians, AL91, PA124,
PA125

Prince Edward Island, PE90

Quebec, QU137

Railroads, IL20, NE48, KY100

Religion*, CA1, DE6,
IL13, IL17, MD26, MA28,
MA32, MA33, PA68

Religious objects, IL14,
IL15, IL18, IA22, MA29,
MA33, MA34, NY55, NY56,
NY64, PA73, PA74, WI82,
WI85

Religious service, AZ138,
  CA139, CO140, CT141,
  DE142, IL143, MD145,
  MA146, MI148, MN149,
  PA158, PA160, PA161,
  TX162, TX163, WI164,
  NB165

Rhode Island, RI129

San Francisco, CA92

Schools, OH116

Scotch-Irish, PA120, PA124,
  PA125, TN131, WV133

Settlement, TX78

Sheet music, PE90

Shillelaghs, NE47, NY55

Shops, NY115, TN131

Silver, MD25, MI40, NY58,
  PA72, PE90

Smoking pipes, MN45

Social movements*, CA1,
  DE8, LA24, MA28

Sod from Ireland, CA2, NY56

Song slides, PA68

South Carolina, SC76

Sports, CA2, MA147, NJ150,
  NY152, OH157, PA161,
  WI164

St. Louis, MO46

St. Patrick's Day, NY114,
  SC130, KY144

Stained glass, MA34, IL99

Stores, NV111

Step dance, AZ138, CO140,
  DE142, Il143, MA146,
  MA147, MI148, NJ150,
  NY151, NY152, PA158,
  PA160, PA161, TX163,
  NB165

Story telling, DC11, NY156,
  OH157, WI164

Structures*, CA1, CA2,
  DE6, DE8, IL12, IL18,
  IL19, LA24, MA28, MA29,
  MA32, MA33, MA36, MA37,
  MA38, NY55, NY62, NY63,
  NC65, OR67, PA74, SC76,
  TX78, WI83, WI84, NF86,
  ON89, MA147

Taverns, DE6, DE8, DC11,
  IL20, LA24, MD26, MA29,
  MA32, MA36, MI40, TX78

Temperance, Il14, MA28

Tennessee, TN131

Texas, TX78, TX79, TX132,
  TX162

Theater, WI164, NB165

Textiles, DE7, PE90, WV133

Textile Tools, MA37, MN45,
  NY63, NC65, WI85

Toilet articles, MA29,
  MN45, WI82

Tools, DE6, DE8, MA29,
  MA37, MN45, NE47, NY63,
  NY64, NC65, PA69, WI82,
  WI83, WI85, NF86

Towns, TX78

Toys and dolls, MA29, MI42,
  PA68, PA73, WI83, WI85

Transportation*, CA1,
  DE8, IL20, LA24, MA29,
  MA36, NY64, PA68, TX78,
  PE90

Travel, ON89

Valley Forge, PA127

Virginia, VA80

Washington, DC, DC98

West Virginia, WV81, WV133

Wisconsin, WI82, WI83, WI84,

(Wisconsin)
  WI85, WI134, WI164

Women, CA1, IL14, WI83,
  CT141

Weapons, CA2, IL14, MA29,
  NE47, WI85

Woodworking tools, MN45,
  NE47, NY64, NC65

About the Compiler

SUSAN K. ELEUTERIO-COMER holds an MA in American Folk Culture from the Cooperstown Graduate Program. She has researched and created museum exhibits and outreach programs about several ethnic groups (including the Irish) in Illinois, New York, and Wisconsin. She is currently a folklife consultant in Chicago.

www.ingramcontent.com/pod-product-compliance
Lightning Source LLC
Chambersburg PA
CBHW060348100426
42812CB00003B/1172

Southern Black
Creative Writers,
1829–1953

Recent Titles in
Bibliographies and Indexes in Afro-American and African Studies

The Afro-American Short Story: A Comprehensive, Annotated Index
with Selected Commentaries
Preston M. Yancy, compiler

Black Labor in America, 1865-1983: A Selected Annotated Bibliography
Joseph Wilson, compiler and editor

Martin Luther King, Jr.: An Annotated Bibliography
Sherman E. Pyatt, compiler

Blacks in the Humanities, 1750-1984: A Selected Annotated Bibliography
Donald Franklin Joyce, compiler

The Black Family in the United States: A Revised, Updated,
Selectively Annotated Bibliography
Lenwood G. Davis, compiler

Black American Families, 1965-1984: A Classified, Selectively Annotated
Bibliography
Walter R. Allen, editor

Index to Poetry by Black American Women
Dorothy Hilton Chapman, compiler

Black American Health: An Annotated Bibliography
Mitchell F. Rice and Woodrow Jones, Jr., compilers

Ann Allen Shockley: An Annotated Primary and Secondary Bibliography
Rita B. Dandridge, compiler

Index to Afro-American Reference Resources
Rosemary M. Stevenson, compiler

A Richard Wright Bibliography: Fifty Years of Criticism and
Commentary, 1933-1982
*Keneth Kinnamon, compiler, with the help of Joseph Benson,
Michel Fabre, and Craig Werner*

Index of Subjects, Proverbs, and Themes in the Writings of Wole Soyinka
Greta M. K. Coger, compiler